The Stud...
to Counse... ...g &
Psychotherapy
Approaches

SAGE has been part of the global academic community since 1965, supporting high quality research and learning that transforms society and our understanding of individuals, groups and cultures. SAGE is the independent, innovative, natural home for authors, editors and societies who share our commitment and passion for the social sciences.

Find out more at: **www.sagepublications.com**

The Student Guide to Counselling & Psychotherapy Approaches

Adrian Pennington

Los Angeles | London | New Delhi
Singapore | Washington DC

Los Angeles | London | New Delhi
Singapore | Washington DC

SAGE Publications Ltd
1 Oliver's Yard
55 City Road
London EC1Y 1SP

SAGE Publications Inc.
2455 Teller Road
Thousand Oaks, California 91320

SAGE Publications India Pvt Ltd
B 1/I 1 Mohan Cooperative Industrial Area
Mathura Road
New Delhi 110 044

SAGE Publications Asia-Pacific Pte Ltd
3 Church Street
#10-04 Samsung Hub
Singapore 049483

Editor: Alice Oven
Assistant editor: Kate Wharton
Production editor: Rachel Burrows
Marketing manager: Tamara Navaratnam
Cover design: Jennifer Crisp
Typeset by: C&M Digitals (P) Ltd
Printed and bound by CPI Group (UK) Ltd,
Croydon, CR0 4YY

Library of Congress Control Number: 2012930

British Library Cataloguing in Publication data

A catalogue record for this book is available from
the British Library

MIX
Paper from
responsible sources
FSC
www.fsc.org   FSC® C013604

ISBN 978-1-4462-4867-6
ISBN 978-1-4462-4868-3 [pbk]

For my family and those I care about

I must thank the following colleagues for their assistance and encouragement in this project: Carole Binysh, Howard Bowman, Penny Cheeseman, Vevi Constantinides, Sandra Flynn, Jan May, Lee Saggers

Contents

About the Author

Adrian has over 5000 hours of supervised clinical experience as a counselling psychologist and performance psychologist, working with individuals, couples, pairs, groups and families. He is a clinical supervisor with more than 20 years' experience, currently supervising eight professional practitioners and students. He is a qualified teacher, and has worked in: secondary education, adult education, youth and community education, further education and higher education, mainly designing and leading counselling certificates and diplomas. He is an ex-Olympic sport psychologist, which included membership of the British Olympic Association Psychology Advisory Group. He is also a qualified mediator.

Adrian has designed, established and managed ten counselling services to date (including in schools, workplace settings, the voluntary sector and the BBC), and has managed two mediation services, as well as authoring a model of family mediation.

How to Use This Guide

The Student Guide is a handy-sized introductory book tightly packed with useful learning and development material, and an easy read.

The aim is to provide a no-frills, concise and uncomplicated summary of some major counselling and psychotherapy approaches for students, practitioners and educators.

It's also directed towards students and professionals from related disciplines who would benefit from an informative and simply-presented resource that gives the streamlined essentials to their knowledge-base. In fact, this little book literally fits inside your pocket. For ease of comparison and contrast of the methodologies described here, each therapeutic chapter is laid out in exactly the same way and at the end of the final chapter a table comprising the approaches and comparative features has been produced for even easier understanding.

The Student Guide begins with an opening chapter about psychology, the discipline from which counselling and psychotherapy have evolved. This introduction includes the origins of the three foundation schools of thought towards reducing, extinguishing and managing human psychological dysfunction, i.e., psychoanalysis, behaviourism/behavioural psychology and humanistic psychology.

One of the major differences between the Student Guide and books of a similar nature is the final chapter, which includes issues and tips such as: a student's own therapy; clinical supervision; charging fees and collecting payment; emergencies; time limits; client non-arrivals/absences; conclusion of the counselling process; boundaries with clients (e.g., friendliness, practitioner self-disclosure).

The remaining 12 chapters offer the reader compact and clear sketches of some of the main counselling and psychotherapeutic approaches chosen for their historical or contemporary impact and relevance.

To make the reading even simpler the chapter sections are explained here:

Origins and Background: in this section the originators, theorists and developers of each approach are introduced along with information about establishing the methodologies, how they evolved, forces which drove some forward and made others stall and the current developments and issues within different perspectives. Thus, the reader can view the approaches in their developmental context.

Some Big Names: some approaches are linked to specific well-known figures but very often there are important people who may not have received the general recognition they deserve. Here, significant players are highlighted along with indicators of their contributions in a couple of sentences each for simple learning and recollection.

Some Big Ideas: each orientation tends to have its own terminology, concepts, techniques and standpoints. So, these are presented in a handy, compact style for straightforward referencing and recall.

How it Works: counselling and psychotherapy are applied disciplines so it's important to see how theory is put into practice. The focus of this section is a practical illustration of how each methodology might tackle the same case of an individual attending for counselling with generalised anxiety. Hopefully, it gives the reader a sense of the similarities and differences between orientations and how they work when implemented with the same client. This aids the understanding of applied theory and method which is vital for all practitioners.

Who it's For: certain approaches are considered to work better with some clients and conditions than others while some are applicable to a wider population. It's helpful for you to know this particularly if you are interested in counselling in specific contexts.

Critical Considerations: over the last 20 years or so there has been a growing interest in, and demand for, evidence of the effectiveness of counselling and psychotherapeutic approaches. But, to be clear, this Guide doesn't have the scope to investigate this area in detail; instead, it aims to provide simple snap-shots of indicators of pros and cons, criticisms of, and evidence for, the methodologies presented in this book. This gives the reader some comprehension of the current status, reputation and usefulness of each orientation.

If you are specifically interested in the area of evidence for counselling approaches there are a number of texts, e.g., Mick Cooper's *Essential Research Findings in Counselling and Psychotherapy* (2011), and L. Timulak's *Research in Psychotherapy and Counselling* (2008).

Identifying Features: it helps to be able to differentiate one approach from another and this section is about what separates each methodology from its peers, presented briefly and straightforwardly in bullet-point fashion.

Reflections: this section is where I share some of my own thoughts, questions and conclusions about each perspective with the reader, which might give them something else to ponder as they develop their own learning and ideas on the included approaches.

Summary: a bite-size précis of each approach is given in 2–4 sentences making memory storage and recall so much simpler for the reader.

Learning Ideas: as an additional dimension individual awareness/developmental challenges and revision topics are included to aid thinking and growth.

Suggested Reading: for easy access, three relevant and contemporary books on the perspective in question (and related topics) are listed at the end of each counselling chapter.

Good reading.

1

In the Beginning...

─────── **Psychology** ───────

Counselling and psychotherapy derive from the mother discipline, psychology. It seems appropriate, therefore, to give a brief introduction to the roots of psychology and its early evolution which led to the emergence and continuing rise of psychological helping and *talking* approaches, some of the most important being introduced in this Guide.

The word *psychology* goes back hundreds of years to such as the Croatian humanist Marko Marulic (1450–1524) and the German philosophers Rudolf Gockel (1547–1628) and Christian Wolff (1679–1754), who further popularised it. *Psychology* comes from the Greek words *psyche*, meaning soul or mind, and *logos* which means word, discourse or reason. The English word *psychology* was introduced in 1693 by Steven Blankaart in his book *The Physical Dictionary*. According to *Webster's Dictionary*, psychology is the study of the soul. *The Oxford Dictionary of Psychology* defines it as 'the study of the nature, functions and phenomena of behaviour and mental experience'. Some describe it as the science of cognitive processes and behaviours (note the lack of reference to emotions...).

William Hamilton (1788–1856) was a Scottish metaphysician who began to use the term *psychology* in preference to *mental philosophy*. This influenced other like-minded thinkers, sowing the seeds of later Western developments in this area (metaphysics is a branch of philosophy that focuses on the fundamentals of *being* and the world).

Actually, recorded interest in the concept and function of the mind and behaviours dates back to the ancient Chinese, Egyptians, Greeks, Indians and Persians.

In its early life psychology was considered a branch of philosophy until the late 19th century when it began to develop as a discipline in its own right, mainly in the USA and Germany. Significant figures at this time included Wilhelm Wundt (1832–1920), a German professor, physician, physiologist and philosopher commonly known as the father of Experimental Psychology. Another was Edward B. Titchener (1867–1927), a British psychologist who studied under Wundt and, like him, was from the Structuralist school of thought, which saw the mind as having structured cognitive processes that could be understood. William James (1842–1910) was an American physician, philosopher and psychologist who became a leader of the Functionalist school of thought, which viewed psychological life in terms of a person's adaptability to their environment, and was a reaction to Structuralism. It also played a part in the rise of behaviourism, as Functionalists believed only scientifically observable behaviours were valid in studying and understanding humans.

As the new discipline of psychology was developing, other influential perspectives on studying and understanding the mind appeared, including mesmerism, the forerunner of hypnosis, presented by Franz A. Mesmer (1734–1815), a German physician. From this, the Scottish physician James Braid (1795–1860) developed hypnosis itself. Phrenology, which claimed the brain was made up of *organs* containing human abilities, faculties and inclinations, also drew much academic interest and study. It was introduced in 1796 by another German physician Franz J. Gall (1758–1828). Phrenologists believed the size and shape of human heads indicate the size of particular organs and the extent of corresponding capabilities or dispositions, and the mind is found within the brain.

During the 19th century the natural sciences of physiology and neurology were moving forward, links being established between certain brain functions, moods and behaviours. The emergence of these two disciplines led to increased research in Experimental Psychology which directly related to the arrival of the first two major psychological therapies, Psychoanalysis and Behaviourism/ Behavioural Psychology (from which Behaviour Therapy evolved). These will now be briefly introduced in order to contextualise the background and emergence of the myriad of resultant counselling and psychotherapeutic theories and approaches.

Psychoanalysis (please see Chapter 11)

This book can only scratch the surface of the foundation discipline of psychological helping; it is a huge area of major contributors, theories, ideas, innovations, developments, perspectives, schools of thought, debates, arguments, criticisms and influences.

Nevertheless, the core concept remains constant, i.e., people can be unaware of what affects their emotions, thoughts and behaviours. Therefore, we can have factors impacting us from our unconscious without knowing it. Negative factors, particularly long-standing or traumatic ones, adversely affect us to varying degrees even to the point of destruction of ourselves and/or others.

3

In psychoanalysis the aim is to bring the unconscious into consciousness, then if we address and understand underlying negative issues and emotions we are in a better position to manage, reduce or resolve them, allowing us to relate better to others, the world and ourselves.

With respect to the many significant names not mentioned here I briefly introduce some of the leading early characters in this most historic of psychological therapies. It begins with the Austrian neurologist Sigmund Freud (1856–1939), who initially proposed the controversial idea that sexual drives are the fundamental motivators in a human's life. He drew on past and topical theories about the unconscious dimension of the mind and its effects on human behaviours and psychological states. He was inspired by the work of the French neurologist Jean-Martin Charcot (1829–1893), who researched into hypnosis. However, Freud used and then rejected hypnosis as ineffective in his psychoanalytical work, seeing *talking cures* as the way forward in reaching and releasing unconscious emotions and thoughts.

Joseph Breuer (1842–1925) was an Austrian physician and colleague of Freud who helped establish psychoanalysis.

Carl G. Jung (1875–1961), a Swiss psychiatrist, was another initial supporter of Freud but separated due to disagreements about some of the basic theories, becoming the founder of Analytical Psychology. He was the first to analyse dreams, and posited ideas like *archetypes*, *complex*, and the *collective unconscious*.

Otto Rank (1884–1939), an Austrian psychoanalyst, was a close colleague of Freud for almost 20 years, helping to battle against internal critics; he became secretary of the Vienna Psychoanalytic Society and then the International Psychoanalytical Association, and was the first to use the term *pre-Oedipal*.

Sandor Ferenczi (1873–1933) was a Hungarian psychoanalyst and ally of Rank; he introduced early *object-relations*

4

ideas and assisted the break from classical psychoanalytical theories and techniques.

Karen Horney (1885–1952), a German-American psychoanalyst, disagreed with Freud about his theories of femininity and worked on psychoanalysis in the context of females; she is now referred to as neo-Freudian.

Melanie Klein (1882–1960) was a British-Austrian psychoanalyst sympathetic to Horney and in disagreement with Freud and his followers. Klein's own school of thought evolved as she developed Child Psychology and became a leader in Object-Relations theory, although she maintained respect for Freud and her theoretical origins.

Donald W. Winnicott (1896–1971), a British paediatrician and psychoanalyst trained by Klein, also helped the development of Object-Relations but later became a more independent thinker. He is influential for concepts like the *true self* and *false self*, and *a holding environment*.

Alfred Adler (1870–1937) was an Austrian physician, psychoanalyst and psychotherapist and another founding member of psychoanalysis. However, he was the first major figure to break away from Freud, producing his own independent personality theory. He introduced the idea of Individual Psychology and proved to have a significant impact on the evolution of counselling and psychotherapy, which is why he is presented at the end of this section, as we view the foundation psychological therapies prior to this Guide's main chapters.

Behaviourism/Behavioural Psychology

The behaviourists wanted to make psychology as scientific as possible and reacted against the other initial schools of thought, denigrating Structuralism, Gestalt Psychology and psychoanalysis even though they shared some common ground with the last two mentioned. The founder is usually recognised as John L. Watson (1878–1958), an American psychologist.

Behaviourism has three core ideas:

1 Psychology is the science of behaviour not the mind.
2 Behaviour can be explained without consideration of internal psychological states and activities.
3 When developing theories in psychology only behavioural concepts and terms should be used.

So, behaviourism developed to the point where it stated that feelings, thought processes and acts could all be regarded as behaviours. Pertaining to this, the behaviourists claimed that only behaviours could be scientifically studied and quantified, and they ignored concepts like emotions, physiological reactions and the mind.

While this may seem quite straightforward and harmonious, there are, indeed, different types of behaviourism that gradually appeared, though there wasn't complete agreement on the factors that distinguished one variation from another, which include:

- Methodical behaviourism: says psychology should only be concerned with overt organismic behaviours in humans and animals, and nothing else; this was the essential proposition of Watson and could also be referred to as *classical behaviourism*.
- Psychological behaviourism: attempts to explain behaviours in terms of our reactions to external stimuli, learning factors and types of reinforcement; it included the work of B.F. Skinner (1904–1990), I. Pavlov (1849–1936) and E. Thorndike (1874–1949).
- Analytical behaviourism: relates to meaning, and semantics of internal thinking and ideas, e.g., if we perceive a person in a certain way, it's due to the way they behave and how they react in situations. The roots lay in logical positivism where meaning is derived from experimental situations or observations that seem to verify their truth.

- Teleological behaviourism: suggests that the best psychological understandings are obtained from objective observations of human behaviours. It acknowledges emotions and cognitions but doesn't accept them as explanations of behaviour. Interestingly, it has a focus on free will and self-control.
- Radical behaviourism: is a way of describing Skinner's approach. It combines elements of the above variations. Since it's concerned with organismic behaviours, it relates to methodical behaviourism. Also, as it views behaviour in terms of stimuli frequency effects and how this impacts cognitions, it connects with psychological behaviourism.

Radical behaviourism claims to be scientific because it uses experimental methods to seek behavioural understanding. Because of Skinner's consideration of emotions, personality and environmental factors like stress, combined with research and experimental analysis of overt behaviours, this approach has also been referred to as *neo-behaviourism.*

In order not to repeat myself, leading names in this movement are referred to in more detail in the Behaviour Therapy chapter (Thorndike, Watson, Skinner). Nevertheless, there are a number of other important contributors to behaviourism, including the following. Clark L. Hull (1884–1952), an American psychologist, was mainly a theoretical behaviourist; he showed his theories could predict and control behaviour. He helped establish *conditioning* as the leading *learning theory* of the age and is famous for his work on *drive theory* (relates to motivation). Drives are forces that activate humans or animals to make behavioural responses. They result from physiological deprivations like water and food, or pain and other unpleasant stimuli.

Edward C. Tolman (1886–1959) was an American psychologist well known for his studies of rats in mazes; he wanted to learn about human psychological functioning by using behavioural experiment.

Richard J. Herrnstein (1930–1994) was an American *Skinnerian* researcher, a founder of *quantitative behavioural analysis* who studied human intelligence. As psychology, psychotherapy and counselling approaches developed in the 20th century, behaviourism in its own right became increasingly sidelined and ultimately rejected as too narrow and restrictive in its understanding and perspective on human beings and how they function. It's been superseded by more expansive and sophisticated theories and methodologies, particularly once the *cognitive revolution* arrived in the 1970s.

In the 21st century the modern version of behaviourism is known as *behaviour analysis* and uses contemporary behavioural learning theory to modify behaviour. Focus areas include mental health, autism, language, verbal behaviours, organisational behaviour management, clinical psychology and cultural psychology.

Humanistic Psychology – 'The Third Force'

Humanistic Psychology came into existence as a strong reaction to psychoanalysis (the First Force) and behaviourism (the Second Force) with their practitioner-led ways of diagnosing, managing and extinguishing human psychological difficulties. Its precursors began to appear in the early years of the 20th century and it was making its mark as a significant school of thought by the 1950s.

Humanistic Psychology drew ideas from such as Eastern philosophies, existentialism, phenomenology and personalism (it speaks philosophically to the uniqueness of the individual human being in the world). The fundamental tenet is that humans are inherently positive beings who, given the appropriate accepting and nurturing environment, will strive to fulfil their essential tendency of reaching their full potential, known as *self-actualisation*.

Without a positively encouraging environment a child will tend to grow in an inhibited manner with a weak *self-concept* (the way we perceive ourselves), and negatively live according to the perceived/assumed demands and expectations of others.

This theoretical perspective inspired a number of therapeutic approaches all based on the idea that people possess the inner resources to heal and grow in a constructive fashion. The aim of therapy is to support clients in removing obstacles to healthier psychological functioning and living.

Some of the leading members of the Third Force are: Gordon W. Allport (1897–1967), an American psychologist and educator who spoke out strongly in his rejection of psychoanalysis and behaviourism, leading the way for others to follow. He emphasised individual human uniqueness and focused on working with a person's present experience instead of their past. He developed *trait theory*, *genotypes* and *phenotypes* (influential internal and external forces that affect behaviour) and was one of the first researchers to distinguish *motives* from *drives*. Allport had much more influence than some give him credit for.

Abraham Maslow (1908–1970) was another American psychologist renowned for his *hierarchy of needs* (physiological; safety; love/belonging; esteem; self-actualisation). He believed in focusing on the positive characteristics of people as opposed to seeing patients/clients as being somehow broken and needing to be fixed by a diagnostic, authoritative outsider. Maslow called his perspective Humanistic Psychology because he and his followers posited that humans have a strong desire to fulfil their positive potential. To evidence this he studied psychologically 'healthy' individuals rather than those with diagnosed psychological issues, conditions or disorders. Maslow's views dovetailed with those of Carl Rogers.

A serious contributor to the foundation of the humanistic movement is Clark Moustakas (born 1923), an American psychologist who researched and wrote about children's play therapy and education. He had discussions with Rogers and Maslow, and helped set up the Association for Humanistic Psychology and the *Journal for Humanistic Psychology*.

Of course, for many, Carl Rogers (1923–1987) is seen as the pre-eminent figure in Humanistic Psychology though such a view would be somewhat unfair to the names above.

Regardless, Rogers is undoubtedly the person acknowledged for setting out the concepts mentioned here in an applied therapeutic manner from which a variety of counselling approaches have developed and related disciplines have benefitted (please see Chapter 10 on Person-Centred Counselling).

2

Behaviour Therapy

======== **Origins and Background** ========

Behaviour Therapy emerged from behavioural psychology, a *scientific* reaction to other early schools of thought prevalent at the turn of the 20th century (please see Chapter 1 for information on Behaviourism). There isn't a clear line where behaviourism ends and Behaviour Therapy begins, since some common experimentation is the foundation of both.

John B. Watson (1878–1958), an American psychologist developed his research and work from the *classical conditioning* studies put forward by the Russian physiologist Ivan P. Pavlov (1849–1936), ultimately forming the basis of Behaviour Therapy. Watson led the behaviourists in rebellion against the other primary psychological perspectives, Gestalt, Structuralism and psychoanalysis. Such *classical* behaviourists considered human beings are 'what they do', postulating that only directly observable behaviour is the single factor worthy of scientific study, and by extension, the way to deal with psychological difficulties.

Around the late 1920s came the rise of the American psychologist and researcher Burrhus F. Skinner (1904–1990) and *operant conditioning*. Skinner based his ideas on his former tutor Charles E.L. Thorndike's (1874–1949) *Reward Learning Theory*. Skinner was a *radical behaviourist*, and, like Watson, didn't believe emotions were important in behaviour and understanding people.

Later, in the UK, Hans J. Eysenck (1916–1997), a German-British psychologist, researched the field of genetics and heredity, and their relationship to intelligence and personality. He found treatments for mental illness, preferring to develop and utilise behavioural therapeutic methods instead of psychoanalysis, which he judged as too slow and sometimes less effective for positive outcomes. He saw behavioural problems as a result of issues between a person's personality, environment and behaviour.

Eysenck became very influential from the 1960s in the UK and Europe, though controversial in certain quarters, being accused of racism for extrapolations he made from some of his findings in the study of intelligence.

From the 1970s cognitive approaches were becoming popular and they often incorporated behavioural techniques. Subsequently, this led to the arrival of the hybrid Cognitive Behaviour Therapy (CBT) which began to gain prominence from the 1990s (please see Chapter 4 on Cognitive Behaviour Therapy).

More recently, Third Generation Behaviour Therapy (also known as *clinical behaviour analysis*) has appeared in a number of forms, e.g. Acceptance and Commitment Therapy, Behavioural Activation, Functional Analytic Psychotherapy. They use principles from classical and operant conditioning, combining them with *functional analysis* and a *clinical formulation* or *case conceptualisation* for work with patients/clients.

Eysenck's definition of Behaviour Therapy became the most used in the UK; it's the attempt to alter human behaviour and emotions in a beneficial way according to the laws of modern learning theory.

Another definition comes from the *Oxford Dictionary of Psychology*, which says Behaviour Therapy is 'A collection of psychotherapeutic techniques aimed at altering maladaptive or unwanted behaviour patterns, especially through the application of principles of conditioning and learning...'.

Behaviour Therapy was designed to treat only learned behavioural problems, which can include a medical dimension/learned medical behaviours. Some of the famous methods include *behaviour modification* (the term usually accredited to E. Thorndike in 1911) which is based on Learning Theory. It involves behaviour change techniques to decrease or increase the frequency of behaviours via *reinforcement* of *adaptive behaviours*. It's also used to extinguish behaviours, and for punishment. A treatment employed for reducing anxiety-related disorders and phobias is *systematic desensitisation*, which derives from a classical conditioning approach. Relaxation techniques are used where clients imagine anxiety-provoking situations in a graduated programme which can ultimately lead to behavioural extinction. Once the imagined events are under control, the method is used in real-life scenarios. Another approach is *flooding* (also known as *exposure therapy*), and, again, comes from classical conditioning. Here, clients with phobias or anxiety disorders (like PTSD (Post Traumatic Stress Disorder)) are exposed to their negative memories and experiences in an attempt to reintegrate repressed emotions into current consciousness. It was introduced by T. Stampfl in 1967.

Some Big Names

Keller, F.S. (1899–1996): American psychologist and educator; friend and colleague of Skinner; he developed the Keller Plan, also known as the Personalised System of Instruction (PSI), a mastery-oriented teaching method which proved very effective with undergraduate students.

Lindsley, O. (1922–2004): American psychologist; he established the Behaviour Research Laboratory at Harvard Medical School, where he analysed behaviours of schizophrenics; given credit for inventing the term Behaviour Therapy, though some attribute this to Skinner.

Mowrer, E.O.H. (1907–1982): American psychologist; his research and work made contemporary Behaviour Therapy more possible; he said any explanation of human behaviour must stand up to common-sense scrutiny....

Wolpe, J. (1915–1997): South African psychiatrist; he was dissatisfied with his results from using psychoanalysis; believed anxieties are learned and treatable via behavioural methods; introduced systematic desensitisation.

Some Big Ideas

Cognitions (thoughts) and emotions are of peripheral importance at best; reward and punishment; reinforcement; aversion therapy; implosion therapy; behavioural experiments; behavioural analysis; self-control training; acceptance and commitment; Dialectical Behaviour Therapy (developed by Marsha Linehan from the 1970s onwards, it also relates to CBT).

How it Works

The approach is used for treating learned behavioural problems, and starts with a client assessment which has three goals:

1 To define and target behavioural problems.
2 To identify cognitions that maintain these behavioural difficulties.
3 Objective measurement of therapeutic/treatment progress (this is checked on a session-by-session basis, and usually involves client self-assessments).

Within this, the practitioner assesses the client for:

- Learned behaviour problems.
- The above plus any unrelated medical issue.
- A learned behaviour problem with a psychosomatic condition.
- Just a medical problem that seems to have been learned.

If progress isn't being made, the practitioner reassesses the client for missed medical or psychiatric conditions, or misunderstanding about the therapy, adjusting the treatment strategy accordingly.

 A brief example

(It's a short-term therapy, so let's imagine this scenario takes eight sessions.)

A new client suffers from anxiety, which affects all areas of their life (late 20s, single, employed full-time, shares a flat with a friend): 'I'm a bit of a worrier.' They want to feel more at ease with themselves and 'not get so stressed about everything'.

You can start by explaining how the therapy works, then get information from the client about what they mean by 'worrier', and what feeling 'more at ease' means in concrete terms, also asking them to clarify 'everything'. From this you can begin to

(Continued)

(Continued)

consider how best to analyse the problems they have in behavioural terms in order to focus on more specific aspects of their condition, and so target where and how to commence behavioural treatment.

While doing this you explore the directly related thought processes that allow the behaviours in question to continue. But remember, the aim is to get to how you're going to treat the client's negative behaviours as quickly as possible. Of course, this doesn't mean you hurry on insensitively; don't rush things, but stay focused on your overall purpose – the extinction of inhibiting behaviours, and replacement with constructive ones.

Once you have understood and analysed the problems (say it takes two sessions to accomplish this) a *clinical formulation* is produced which is essentially the strategy for eliminating undesired behaviours, replacing them with desirable ones. Needless to say, the client has to be committed to the actions that follow for successful outcomes to be achieved. Progress can be appraised by client self-measurement assessments conducted during each session, which are intended to be both evidential and positively reinforcing, showing the benefits of the *behavioural experiments* being undertaken. When doing this it's imperative for you to be empathic towards the client – work hard not to sound or look critical if the client is struggling with a piece of homework.

Let's suppose the first part of the plan concerns changing behaviours relating to the client's avoidance of large weekly staff meetings. They say being in big groups causes anxiety which affects their ability to think straight and express their views coherently. This makes them worried about showing themselves up and being criticised so they try and find feasible reasons not to attend. Recently, colleagues have started to comment about the client's increasing absences, and this simply makes the client more anxious and strengthens their desire to avoid the next meeting. They know things can't continue in this downward spiral but are uncertain about their capacity to remedy the situation, which simply makes them worry even more.

Your clinical formulation addresses this particular issue first. The plan is that the client will go to the next meeting even if they don't actively participate by talking at the event. Attendance will equal success. Before they go in they will practise becoming calmer by using a breathing exercise you teach them, another form of behaviour change.

The client attends the meeting on time, doesn't speak on any issue and stays until the end. Over subsequent weeks the client goes regularly, thus exposing themselves to anxiety-provoking situations, still not speaking. Yet, consistent attendance means measurable progress is being made; in effect, they are modifying their behaviours. You point this out to the client every time they report to you in session, so positively reinforcing their actions and new powers of *self-control*. Remember not to be overly positive as that can come across as patronising or disingenuous – monitor yourself and get the correct balance.

Gradually, via this approach, your client's anxiety levels are managed better and decrease to the point where they are ready to say something in a meeting. This is practised at home beforehand and involves giving a verbal greeting to one person when they arrive. Things continue at this level until the client is ready to say 'Hello' to a second person, and so on. Their self-assessment of progress is checked at every session, including the evidence of success (attending more meetings, then actually saying something) which underlines the effectiveness of the work. The agreed ultimate aim from this behavioural progression is to prepare one thing to say at a large staff meeting so proving to the client that success can be achieved via focusing on specific behavioural changes, and not on unhelpful thoughts and emotions. By employing this graduated procedure, client anxiety levels are reduced and negative behaviours become inhibited as new desirable behaviours are established, maintained, measured and reinforced.

Who it's For

Behaviour Therapy has been used in the psychological health sphere for many years, e.g., most phobias, OCD (Obsessive Compulsive Disorder), sexual problems, stammering; in the educational field to improve child/pupil/student behaviours, e.g., behaviour modification in school classroom settings, social skills training; bed-wetting; sleeping problems; it's utilised with people of all ages and is the core methodology for animal training.

The approach is less likely to work with those who drink too much, are on strong medication, who have major psychological health/medical conditions, or are particularly low on motivation.

Critical Considerations

There's still no generally accepted learning theory to support Eysenck's definition, though there are ongoing attempts to provide one.

Some criticise the therapy as deriving from a one-dimensional perspective of human beings, and consider it unrealistic for having this view.

Much of the early research evidence for the approach's efficacy comes from animal experimental studies, the findings being generalised to human beings.

J.B. Watson has been criticised for 'selling' behaviourism and its therapeutic methods via his personality and writings, not scientifically through the provision of research evidence.

Another criticism is that Behaviour Therapy theory doesn't fully explain avoidance learning or some effects of punishment on learning.

Identifying Features

The approach sees behaviour as the defining characteristic of being human; thinking and emotions are unimportant; research-based; a foundation stone of the later Cognitive Behaviour Therapy; typically employed in short-term work.

Reflections

Behaviour Therapy's origins go right back to the beginnings of the core discipline, psychology, in a period of emerging perspectives and schools of thought. The behaviourists were determined to make psychology scientific in order to increase its credibility. They were rebellious, undermining other standpoints and emphasising their own superiority. Certainly, they were different, often being described as radical, with their claims that only behaviours really counted in the therapeutic sphere. However, as the counselling field has grown so significantly over the last 100 years, there are many practitioners, theorists and researchers who view this once-radical and edgy force as something now rather narrow and outmoded. I believe Behaviour Therapy is too simplistic to convincingly explain the complex makeup of human beings and how to assist better psychological functioning. I think this can be evidenced by the relatively rapid rise of other modalities. So, even with a broader perspective, Behaviour Therapy is, in my view, under increasing pressure from more encompassing approaches such as the cognitive behaviour therapies, e.g., Rational Emotive Behaviour Therapy (REBT), Cognitive Analytical Therapy (CAT), and even Developmental Counselling.

Also, if behaviour therapists have joined with cognitive therapists, even tacitly, then surely that indicates this long-standing methodology is acknowledging that its historical theoretical narrowness and inherent limitations have had their day?

It's clear in more modern behavioural literature that the emotional and cognitive dimensions of human functioning are anything but peripheral in terms of their importance in therapeutic settings. Moreover, defining humans as 'what they do' is surely too unrealistic, simplistic, or even just plain wrong?

Nevertheless, we should note the concepts and techniques that have been incorporated into other approaches and their relative success with certain mental health conditions.

Summary

Behaviour Therapy emerged from the early behavioural school of psychology which was attempting to be the dominant force in making the discipline more scientific. Behaviourists contended that only overt behaviours are worthy of recognition, those concerning the inhibition and extinction of maladaptive behaviours which negatively impact our lives. It's been ostracised in a number of quarters but has proved useful for combating such as depression, OCD and ADHD (Attention Deficit Hyperactivity Disorder), particularly in formal mental health contexts, sometimes gaining better results than, say, cognitive or psychodynamic approaches.

Overall, though, it appears traditional orthodox Behaviour Therapy is being superseded by newer, more comprehensive and sophisticated modalities.

Learning Ideas

1   Design a behavioural treatment programme to aid an imaginary client with OCD to overcome an unwanted behaviour: every time they leave home they check the front door is firmly closed by pushing on it 24 times before they can go on their way. Work out how you would help this client make progress (remember, it must be measurable). Set it out on a piece of A4.

2   Reflect on yourself: what are your behavioural habits or inclinations when you feel stressed, and how might you extinguish them using a behavioural approach?

3   Revision

   a   Make sure you know and understand about Dialectical Behaviour Therapy and Third Generation Behaviour Therapies, and how they relate to orthodox Behaviour Therapy.

   b   Know the difference between a compulsion and an obsession.

   c   Think of an example of classical conditioning and one of operant conditioning so you are clear about the differences between them.

 ## Suggested Reading

Barlow, D.H. and Craske, M.G. (2009) *Mastery of Your Anxiety and Panic*. Oxford: Oxford University Press.

Jena, S.P.K. (2008) *Behaviour Therapy: Techniques, Research, Applications*. London: Sage.

Swales, M.A. and Heard, H.L. (2009) *Dialectical Behaviour Therapy*. Hove: Routledge.

3

Cognitive Analytical Therapy (CAT)

Origins and Background

CAT was introduced in the late 1970s and is the brain-child of Anthony Ryle, a psychiatrist and analytical psychotherapist. He was working in the UK's National Health Service and found traditional psychoanalysis too slow for addressing patients' psychological issues and conditions. He concluded that a faster, more direct, active, effective, cost-conscious and collaborative therapy was the way forward for patients within the system. Ryle also wanted an approach that clients could understand, learn and then use to manage themselves better. Ryle wished to take the approach to the wider population, too.

This integrated therapeutic method combines features from two main standpoints in a single structured framework. First, CAT takes aspects from cognitive psychology and Cognitive Therapy, an important part coming from personal construct theory, i.e., we construct our realities from how we perceive experiences in our lives and subsequent assumptions we make. It also includes the idea that our connected thoughts, beliefs and behaviours are a fundamental source of how we view and live life (it should be briefly noted at this point that CAT also takes aspects from the broader Cognitive Behaviour Therapy).

Secondly, the approach is psychoanalytical with an emphasis on early relationship formations and their later impact on future relationships; it also refers to the relevance of the *conscious* and *unconscious*, and orientates towards the *object-relations* view of how to understand human relational dynamics. So, for a CAT practitioner the impact of early influences on clients is a major focus area.

CAT is known as the Procedural Sequence Object Relations Model (PSORM), and for practitioners a major focus will be on past and present relationships and how they can affect a person's future interpersonal dynamics. Briefly then, negative relationships, dynamics and attachments when we are young affect the development of our maladaptive thinking and formation of underlying (perhaps unconscious) irrational and undesirable beliefs about ourselves, and assumptions about our world, which lead us to act and relate in inhibiting ways.

CAT posits that client issues arise from the continued operation of unchanged inhibiting *procedural sequences* which imprint on them ways to respond to difficult environmental and interpersonal situations.

Within the approach, the practitioner's role is a key factor, as is how they view clients. Fundamentally, they see client relationships with other people as stemming from what has been learnt from key figures when the client was young. In other words, clients learn to do to themselves what has been done to them in the past by significant adults. Similarly, they do for themselves what these people have done for them when they were younger. With this perspective operating, the practitioner re-educates clients, showing them a broader view of any way they have been unhelpfully affected by others, e.g., low self-esteem, depression, self-hatred, defensiveness, anxiety, sensitivity to perceived criticism.

Relating to this, CAT practitioners work to be aware of what clients might subconsciously expect from the therapeutic dynamic, e.g., if a client has a powerful critical parent figure in their lives, one who guides, instructs, criticises, then they might expect the practitioner to act in a similar manner. This is called a client *self-state* and people may have a number of them. If the practitioner doesn't behave in a fashion consistent with the client's expectations, establishing rapport and trust might need some extra sensitivity, along with a clear explanation of the practitioner's role. Indeed, with patients who have serious personality disorders, the practitioner's task may be a greater challenge, especially if they attempt to maintain a degree of neutrality and not be drawn into playing roles the client may want or expect from them. The aim is to get to a point where the two parties can work collaboratively, rather than the client being led by a decision-making authority figure, like it's always been with, say, the client's parent, which is what the term *reciprocal role procedure* refers to. While practitioner empathy is an important attribute, so is the strength and self-discipline to stay in role and not become the 'parent' – that will simply undermine desired outcomes because the client will continue in the subordinate child mode.

CAT requires the practitioner to be focused, organised, assertive in maintaining their position, and able to empower clients by the skilful use of psycho-educational interventions. Students of this approach need to be particularly well grounded in psychoanalytical/dynamic and cognitive/cognitive behavioural theory and practice.

Some Big Names

Bakhtin, M.M. (1895–1975): Russian philosopher and semiotician (relates to linguistics); he worked on the philosophy of language;

introduced the concept of dialogism (analysing meaning in communication).

Brown, A.L. (1943–1999): British educational psychologist; he assisted the development of *scaffolding* to promote learning and skills acquisition.

Vygotsky, L.S. (1896–1934): Russian psychologist; into developmental psychology, child development, education; he presented the idea of the Zone of Proximal Development.

 Some Big Ideas

Target problem procedures; reformulation letter; the Psychotherapy File; traps/dilemmas/snags; Socratic questions; homework; diary; client diagrams; dialogism/Dialogical Sequence Analysis; recognition; revision; goodbye letters; exits.

How it Works

The number of sessions can range between six and 24, excluding follow-ups; a common session number is 16, which is utilised for this section.

The aim of the therapy is for practitioner and client to discover inhibiting behavioural patterns, then introduce, practise and maintain alternative ways of living, in order to function better.

Put simply, the process can be divided into four parts:

Phase 1: Reformulation (first four sessions): this is when the client explains what brings them into counselling; life story; general informational details; current situation; main issues; looking for any underlying repetitive negative procedures in their relationships. To help the client learn about themselves, the Psychotherapy File is introduced in the first session, and in the rest of this part the *client diagram* concept appears to assist in illustrating *problem procedures*, and aids the production of the formulation letter which the practitioner writes at the end of the fourth session (it is basically a type of assessment from which the practitioner considers potential ways forward). During this period the practitioner is also working to establish a sound therapeutic relationship with the client, plus explaining CAT perspectives and principles, and how the process works.

Phase 2: Recognition (usually four sessions): this is when the client can use a diary to help recognise negative relational patterns, which they discuss with the practitioner prior to enacting desired changes (e.g., spotting the reciprocal roles they play with other people). This can involve considering the *traps*, *dilemmas* and *snags* which undermine them.

Phase 3: Revision (the remaining eight of the 16 sessions): both parties collaborate on material from the formulation letter, adapting it if necessary, identifying and practising *exits* from historical negative action patterns, moving towards new and constructive thinking and behaviours, and greater client self-belief.

Phase 4: Goodbye letters: the practitioner essentially produces a written summary of what's happened in the process from beginning to end; it might also include concerns or areas to work on for the client in the future; dates for (two) follow-up sessions are included. Some clients decide to write an exit letter for the practitioner as their way of ending the relationship.

 A brief example

A new client suffers from anxiety, which affects all areas of their life (late 20s, single, employed full-time, shares a flat with a friend): 'I'm a bit of a worrier.' They want to feel more at ease with themselves and not get so 'stressed about everything'.

Let's say everything starts off smoothly with you informing the client of the theory and practice of CAT, your role and the part to be played by the client. Session 1 seems to go well, with apparently positive feedback from the client about the initial experience at the end. But, in the next meeting the client appears to distance themselves from you when they claim not to know why they feel so anxious and lacking in confidence and you don't give them the answers.

This is when you need to be using high-quality basic counselling skills and empathy, trying to get the client to understand and accept you're not their parent, and so are not their guide, director or judge. In other words, you provide some psycho-education, explaining about your client's *reciprocal role procedures* and how this pertains to their early-years relationship development with their critical parent and other authority figures.

Gradually, by your sensitive firmness, the client adopts a more appropriate form of relating with you. They take on the tasks of homework and the Psychotherapy File, contributing to the ingredients of the Sequential Diagrammatic Reformulation (SDR) and helping to target their *problem procedures*. From this comes your assessment or *reformulation letter* and you both proceed to the Recognition phase, which includes discussing their early attachments, the client learning about the impact of the unconscious, parental attachments and the use of inhibiting traps, dilemmas and snags.

Part of the progress here relates to the concept of *scaffolding*, which essentially means you teach the client new ways of thinking and behaving, and how to *exit* from their negative ways to maintain and develop constructive changes. The idea is that the client takes them on in order to support themselves and become more rationally self-managing once the counselling has finished. This is what happens in Phase 3 when cognitive and behavioural revision occurs for the client before arriving at the therapeutic conclusion where you produce your exit letter.

You remember to inform the client they have the option of writing their own exit letter to you, but stress that there is no compunction or expectation that they should do this. It needs to be a free choice on their part. They decide not to, but agree to two follow-up sessions.

Who it's For

CAT was developed within the UK National Health system but aims to be adaptable to the needs of a general population.

It's employed with younger people and adults; couples; groups; those with learning disabilities, and across cultures.

The method is used for issues such as anxiety/panic; depression; self-harm; a range of psychological health conditions and disorders; relationship difficulties. However, it isn't usually applicable for psychotic patients, or for people who have serious issues with drugs and/or alcohol.

In recent years CAT has focused on working with serious psychological health conditions, such as personality disorders.

Critical Considerations

CAT aims to assist people for whom other therapies have been unsuccessful or of limited help. While this is a laudable ambition, the long-term usefulness of the approach is yet to be proven, but some research studies are currently under way. Being a new methodology, CAT hasn't yet received in-depth systematic reviews of its efficacy, but has been the subject of randomised controlled trials, involving subjective client ratings relating to the treatment they have had. Such evaluations have indicated support for the approach in the areas of anorexia, diabetes management, some brain injuries, self-harm, dissociative psychosis, dissociative identity disorder, histrionic personality disorder, and more needs to be conducted.

Relating to this, a criticism is that short-term approaches may frustrate and even de-motivate patients with long-term personality disorders, possibly compounding their conditions.

Some of CAT's terminology has been accused of being confusing rather than clarificatory, bearing in mind that it wants to be an approach readily learned and understood by as many people as possible.

Identifying Features

The reformulation letter concept (a theoretically-based explanation of a client via information obtained from a clinical assessment); exit letters; client diagrams; modelling; a new short-term, integrated structured methodology; practice is based in the mental health sphere though it's now becoming used with a wider client population; rejects the idea of defence mechanisms.

Reflections

CAT is establishing itself as a prominent methodology, integrating ideas from psychodynamic and cognitive (behavioural) perspectives. It's currently attempting to bring improved operations and understanding to the area of serious psychological dysfunction within the institutional mental health field, and this is now its main focus, apparently.

CAT has also been taken to the wider general population and is increasingly practised in the UK and Europe.

I think it has some interesting concepts, such as the reformulation and exit letters, and client diagrams (also known as Sequential Diagrammatic Reformulations, SDRs), which make it stand in its own right, but also has similarities to schema-focused CBT, where differences are seen by some as little more than matters of emphasis. However,

I think the importance given to the psychodynamic dimension of CAT is enough to differentiate it from CBT.

Another interesting aspect is the CAT view of where client issues arise, i.e., *between* people, rather than *inside* an individual.

Given the financial restrictions around funding to discover evidence for its use and the popularity of CBT within health-related institutions, CAT is nevertheless finding its place in the range of therapeutic approaches within the cognitive behavioural family.

Summary

CAT was designed as a short-term, psycho-educational method; it's a new integrated approach, based in the mental health system, more recently focusing on serious psychological conditions. It's founded on psychoanalytical/psychodynamic and cognitive/cognitive behavioural principles. While still in need of evidence to support its effectiveness, this therapy is steadily becoming recognised as a significant addition to the family of counselling approaches since its arrival in the late 1970s.

Learning Ideas

1   Think about CAT's rejection of the concept of defence mechanisms. Read and consider the arguments 'for' and 'against' the CAT position, write them down, and include your own conclusions.

2   Be honest with yourself and reflect on your own traps, dilemmas and snags, and what you could do about them.

3   Revision

  a Make certain you know how and when to use: reformulation letters; client diagrams; Psychotherapy File.

b Make sure you understand: reciprocal role procedure; procedural sequences; scaffolding; modelling.

c Check your knowledge and comprehension of fundamental psychoanalytical/dynamic and cognitive/cognitive behavioural concepts, and how they relate to CAT theory and practice.

Suggested Reading

Denman, F. (1995) Treating Eating Disorders Using Cognitive Analytical Therapy: Two Case Examples. In A. Ryle (ed.), *Cognitive Analytical Therapy: Developments in Theory & Practice*. Chichester: John Wiley & Son.

Hepple, J. and Sutton, S. (2004) *Cognitive Analytical Therapy and Later Life*. Hove: Brunner-Routledge.

Ryle, A. and Kerr, I. (2002) *Introducing Cognitive Analytical Therapy: Principles and Practice*. Chichester: John Wiley & Sons.

4

Cognitive Behaviour Therapy (CBT)

From the outset, it's important to note that the term *CBT* is more than a single therapy, there being a number of cognitive behavioural approaches, e.g., Rational Emotive Behaviour Therapy (REBT); Cognitive Therapy; Cognitive Analytical Therapy (CAT); the Developmental Approach.

That said, there are now fairly standardised courses where ideas, procedures, techniques, etc., are taught to students, giving a general foundation to this rapidly emerging methodology.

CBT is the result of a merger between Cognitive Therapy and Behaviour Therapy, combining *cognitive restructuring* ideas and *behaviour modification* techniques. Some people call it a talking therapy, while others refute this, describing it as an action-oriented approach. I think it could be described as both talk and action-based. It would be accurate to define it as *a systematic goal-focused procedure*. It is often brief or time-limited, say between six and 20 sessions, and is used in both individual and group settings.

CBT has three underlying assumptions:

1   Thinking determines emotions and behaviours.
2   Negative thinking can become a habit and may lead to significant emotional difficulties and disorders if thinking is

extreme and/or continuously negative, i.e., if it's a norm for someone.

3 Learning to think more constructively and realistically can result in less emotional negativity and better client functioning in the future.

The successful completion of behavioural tasks can be strong evidence to people about defeating negative thinking and beliefs, i.e., constructive change is possible.

The idea of *automatic thoughts* put forward by Aaron Beck is important here; he gave this name to negative cognitions and images that involuntarily occur in a person's mind. Albert Ellis stressed the part played by *irrational beliefs* underpinning negative thinking, which may be significant in leading to psychological dysfunction, inhibiting us from reaching goals and fulfilling potential. Ellis suggested three main irrational beliefs:

1 I must win approval from others, otherwise I'm worthless.
2 People must treat me in the way I want them to, otherwise they are wrong, and should be blamed and punished.
3 Life must give me all I want when I want it, and give me nothing I don't want.

Later, in his work with M.E. Bernard, Ellis said these irrational beliefs can result in three types of self-defeating thinking found in clients with emotional disorders:

1 I'm worthless because...
2 It's awful that...
3 I can't stand it that...

Another important contributor to what became CBT was A. Lazarus (born 1932) who developed *broad-spectrum* CBT, from the 1950s to the 1970s. His ideas included taking note of physical sensations, visual images, biological factors, interpersonal relationships and dynamics. This work led directly on to his Multi-Modal Therapy, where *modalities* – feeling, acting, sensing, imagining, interacting – formed the basis of the counselling process.

This work is structured around the BASIC ID idea: **B**ehaviour; **A**ffect; **S**ensation; **I**magery; **C**ognition; **I**nterpersonal relationships; **D**rugs/biology, indicating Lazarus's belief that therapy should heed more than thinking and actions. His contribution helped the progress of cognitive approaches, also opening up dialogue possibilities with behaviourists.

CBT is a growing methodology with a range of spin-offs falling under the general heading (e.g., Cognitive Processing Therapy; Computerised CBT; and please see below).

Some Big Names

Bandura, A. (born 1925): American psychologist; he helped develop social learning theory, and later, Social Cognition Theory (SCT), in the 1980s.

Glasser, W. (born 1925): American psychiatrist; he developed Choice Theory and Reality Therapy, a CBT approach.

Low, A. (1891–1954): American neuro-psychiatrist; he worked and experimented in the treatment of mental illness, devising patient self-help programmes.

Mischel, W. (born 1930): American psychologist; he helped develop SCT, which was behaviourally based with a strong cognitive dimension.

Some Big Ideas

Cognitive distortions; low frustration tolerance (LFT); cognitive assessment; cognitive intervention; ABC theory; case formulation; homework; practitioner redundancy.

How it Works

The CBT practitioner educates clients, teaching them to:

- Monitor and observe events that set off negative emotional reactions.
- Explore and identify negative thought patterns and underlying beliefs.
- Make links between negative thinking, emotions and behaviours.
- Test out negative thinking and beliefs, and consider the evidence for and against them.
- Replace negative thinking (and behaviour) with new constructive cognitive processes, integrating them via practice so clients become better self-managers with reduced negativity.

Often clients are unaware of their unhelpful thinking habits in relation to how they feel, and need a safe environment and sensitive practitioner interventions to see and understand their cognitive patterns. It's important the client is given the opportunity and responsibility of deciding to do something about their issues; some will 'talk the talk' but not 'walk the walk'. From this, goals are agreed and set. Then the practitioner educates the client about how to change maladaptive thinking; the idea is to aid the client find evidence to disprove their negative cognitions and beliefs in order to change them for constructive thinking. Behavioural tasks are discussed and carried out in search for the evidence just mentioned.

At this stage the practitioner's job involves engaging the client in a process of change, and teaching them about the theory and practice of change. Thus the client becomes better equipped to manage themselves more constructively in the future, resolving their own difficulties, and the practitioner is ultimately made redundant.

It's important for the client to understand the ABC format, which is a significant tool of CBT, crucial to client assessments and practitioner interventions:

- **A** (**a**ctivating event): this can be an actual situation or the result of imagining what will happen within such an event.
- **B** (underlying **b**eliefs): these could be viewed as internal client mini-theories; they may be correct or incorrect, founded on what the client perceives as evidence for thinking in such ways. They can be difficult to shift so the practitioner needs patience.
- **C** (emotional and behavioural **c**onsequences of **B**): these can be expected or anticipated, usually based on previous experiences.

It's common for clients to think in terms of an A–C formula, i.e., the activating event causes the consequences. This can be investigated via the use of an ABC assessment conducted by the practitioner, and indicates the role of Bs.

The aim here is to help the client understand that Cs are not the consequences of the activating events, As, but rather they stem from negative cognitions and beliefs, Bs. This lays the groundwork for the formulation of behavioural tasks which will undermine evidence for the client's negative cognitions, imaginings and beliefs.

Some of the techniques/tasks include: behavioural homework assignments; cognitive rehearsal work; writing a journal/diary; modelling; conditioning; systematic desensitisation; validity testing.

The steps of the ABC assessment are:

1   Assess the C.
2   Assess the A.
3   Understand the link between A and C.
4   Assess B.
5   Link B and C.

A brief example

(Say 12 sessions.)

A new client suffers from anxiety, which affects all areas of their life (late 20s, single, employed full-time, shares a flat with a friend): 'I'm a bit of a worrier.' They want to feel more at ease with themselves and 'not get so stressed about everything'.

You meet with the client and during the first two or so sessions you employ basic counselling skills and core conditions to establish the foundations of the therapeutic relationship. The initial objective includes understanding what brings them to you, and their issues. From this you are in a better position to observe the client, listen to them, earn trust, explore and understand their negative thinking and beliefs. This helps when it comes to producing your *case formulation*.

Suppose the client quickly has rapport with you and tells you about an up-coming event which is making them very anxious. You must be prepared to modify the case formulation, if necessary, as they explain the situation.

The client informs you they have to sit a formal exam as part of a qualification they're taking. If successful, they will be promoted at work. You both explore the thoughts and images about the exam. Although the client has always been academically capable, as they've got older their confidence has waned, replaced by anxiety about such activities. You discover underlying beliefs about the client not being good enough without guidance from their parent, and that colleagues will consider the client a failure unless they are continually achieving. The client worries their anxiety will lead to exam failure.

Preparation for the exam becomes the focus for the next few sessions. This involves the client keeping a journal of daily negative

(Continued)

37

(Continued)

thought and producing more rational alternatives; finding and reading their previous exam certificates, and reminding themselves of the history of their academic achievements, including the successes gained on their current course, which they are doing well in. Such exercises are *validation tests* about the client's ability to achieve on their own, counteracting in-built negative beliefs.

Additionally, you conduct some positive visualisation work in the sessions to assist the client to imagine themselves arriving for the exam in a confident frame of mind and competently producing answers. The client learns how to breathe more calmly and focus on positive images relating to the exam. Together you construct a set of preparation steps relating to the exam build-up (e.g., what time to stop revising the night before; what to do when preparing for bed that night; calmness and visualisation work; sleeping soundly; waking refreshed and confident; getting ready and checking they have all they need; travel plan for arrival at the venue; waiting prior to exam time; entering the room; sitting and waiting; reading the exam paper carefully and calmly; making initial notes; writing answers). These steps are incorporated into the weekly visualisation exercise and the validation tests are discussed. Of course, what's happening is the client focuses on what to do to achieve rather than worrying about what could go wrong.

As sessions progress *cognitive shifts* occur, with the client thinking, behaving and reporting to you in a more realistic manner, becoming fairer with themselves. You monitor, check and support their progress.

Consequently, client confidence grows as greater belief in their abilities develops, replacing negative cognitions with constructive ones. When the day of the exam arrives the client is thinking more realistically, recognising their talents and is composed, prepared to perform well.

Who it's For

CBT is used for such as affective (mood) disorders, e.g., bipolar disorder; personality disorders; schizophrenia; eating disorders; substance misuse; anxiety; panic disorder; agoraphobia; Obsessive Compulsive Disorder (OCD); social phobia; clinical depression; Post Traumatic Stress Disorder (PTSD); Attention Deficit Hyperactivity Disorder (ADHD); chronic pain; rheumatoid arthritis; back problems; sleep disorders; cancer. Sometimes, therapy is accompanied by medication.

Currently, in the UK, CBT is the therapy which underpins the IAPT (Improved Access to Psychological Therapies) initiative in the National Health Service (NHS).

CBT may be inappropriate for severely psychotic patients and cognitively impaired people, e.g., those with organic brain conditions or brain injuries.

Within prison populations, CBT has been effective in modifying offender thinking patterns. It's also used in other settings, e.g., education, the workplace.

The approach is employed with children and adults.

For those wanting insight into their past, or to explore their way of being, they might be more suited to other modalities, e.g., psychodynamic, Person-Centred, Gestalt Therapy.

Critical Considerations

Some CBT students and practitioners from other perspectives think the therapeutic relationship is unimportant in this approach. They are mistaken; good CBT practitioners continually monitor their dynamics with clients throughout the process. Another misconception is that CBT is all about 'positive thinking', but the method is actually about helping people think more constructively, realistically, rationally.

The approach is criticised because some practitioners and contractors insist on providing only a minimum number of sessions while clients may need longer-term work.

The argument as to whether the approach is defined as a talk or action therapy seems rather superfluous to many of us since it's obviously a combination of both.

The idea of contract sanctions and rewards is open to criticism for reasons mentioned below.

There has been formal research evidencing the approach and it's currently supported in the UK by the National Institute for Health and Clinical Excellence (NICE). However, some suggest the evidence isn't yet enough to warrant the strength of support and finance CBT receives.

Identifying Features

A self-help, usually short-term approach (say 6–10 sessions, sometimes up to 20); skills training; psycho-educational; a hybrid methodology; practitioner redundancy.

Reflections

The issue of contracts is an interesting one. There are some practitioners, e.g., from a behavioural background, who try to make 'formal' contracts which include sanctions or penalties if there is a breach of this agreement.... What does that mean? What penalties do we have the authority to impose? Apparently, rewards are given if clients stick with the contract.... Again, what does this mean? Whatever the answer, to me it seems to imply the practitioner is in a real power-position.

Not everyone knows or appreciates that CBT practitioners, if well taught, are educated not only to learn the procedures, techniques, etc., but to develop their own therapeutic style. I think this is a particularly important piece of information for you to remember.

In my experience, there are still 'old school' lecturers and tutors on CBT training courses who remain rather behaviour-based, down-playing emotions and certain techniques, e.g., the visualisation example given above.

Overall, I think CBT has much to offer, being a logical merger of Cognitive and Behaviour Therapies, and is certainly 'flavour of the month' at the time of writing this book, especially in the UK Health Service – but, remember, that doesn't mean it's perfect because there is no ideal counselling approach...

===== **Summary** =====

CBT has rapidly established itself as a significant methodology in the UK and elsewhere. It integrates major elements of the cognitive and behavioural viewpoints. Students are taught the main principles, practices, techniques, but should be encouraged to develop their own style within the major ideas and guidelines. It has supportive evidence but question marks remain over the long-term effects of what's fundamentally a short-term approach.

Learning Ideas

1 Consider steps you might take in a case formulation relating to a female client who gets very stressed when she is about to engage in sexual activity. She wants to overcome the anxiety, for herself and her partner's sake. Write down how you could engage the client and how you would build rapport and trust with her. Think about what techniques and tasks might be useful in such cases.

2 The ABC format: what are your As, Bs and Cs? Be honest!

3 Revision

   a Know the basics of the following: Social Learning Theory; Social Cognition Theory; Choice Theory; Reality Therapy.

   b Check the meaning and your understanding of these terms: modelling; cognitive rehearsal; validity testing.

   c Learn about breathing techniques for use with clients.

 ## Suggested Reading

Bond, F.W. and Dryden, W. (2004) *Handbook of Brief Cognitive Behaviour Therapy*. Chichester: Wiley.

Mayer, M.J., van Acker, R., Lochman, J.E. and Gresham, F.M. (2009) *Cognitive Behavioural Interventions for Emotional and Behavioural Disorders: School-Based Practice*. New York: Guilford Press.

Trower, P., Casey, A. and Dryden, W. (2002) *Cognitive Behavioural Counselling in Action*. London: Sage.

5

Cognitive Therapy

Aaron T. Beck, an American medical doctor, psychiatrist and psychoanalyst, is regarded as the founder of this approach (born in 1921; he became particularly prominent from the 1960s). He was partly motivated by George Kelly's ideas, mentioned below. We must also note here that Beck worked closely with another important theorist and practitioner, Albert Ellis, who went on to introduce Rational Emotive Behaviour Therapy (REBT).

Much of Beck's early work focused on the treatment of clinical depression via cognitive methods. Later, he concluded that anxiety is a core human emotion and began to develop cognitive treatments accordingly.

As a researcher, Beck was interested in evidencing the impact of cognitive techniques, the result being a number of assessment schedules including the Beck Depression Inventory and the Beck Anxiety Inventory. The idea of schedules came about from his early experiments to test psychoanalytical factors of depression, which brought poor results, and so he considered other ways of conceptualising this condition before moving on to studying anxiety. He found patients had what he termed *automatic thoughts*, saying this type of thinking fell into three categories:

1 Negative ideas about oneself.
2 Negative ideas about the world and existence.
3 Negative ideas about the future.

From this, Beck helped patients identify and evaluate these negative thoughts which led to more realistic thinking, resulting in improved emotional states and better functioning behaviours. In the 1990s he concluded that negative automatic thinking reveals a person's core beliefs, which result from life-long experiences.

Cognitive Therapy is underpinned by the belief that psychological distress is caused by distorted thinking in patients/ clients. The approach makes the assumption that false *self-beliefs* lead to negative emotions and behaviours. The therapy aims to assist clients in recognising and reassessing patterns of negative thinking, replacing them with constructive cognitive processes more closely reflecting reality.

One of Beck's key concepts is *schemas*; he said we have assumptions underlying our perceptions of reality and the rules we live by. These schemas are learnt from our major socialising agents and may be firmly in place as early as eight years of age. They can be personal, religious, gender-based, cultural, family-based, and are viewed for the purposes of predicting cognitive, emotional and behavioural reactions, forming the foundation of client automatic thoughts and the practitioner's understanding of these negative thinking habits.

Cognitive Therapy describes 10 common faulty thinking patterns, known as *cognitive distortions*:

1 All-or-nothing Thinking: using 'absolute' language like 'never', 'always', 'forever'.
2 Over-generalisation: referring to a single case then assuming all others will be the same.

3 Mental Filter: focusing on negatives in life, ignoring/filtering out positives.
4 Disqualifying the Positive: saying they don't really count.
5 Jumping to Conclusions: assuming the worst even though there's no evidence to support this thinking.
6 Emotional Reasoning: emotions dominate our ability to think rationally.
7 Magnification and Minimisation: downplaying positives, emphasising negatives.
8 'Should' Statements: focusing on how we think we/others/the world/the future/life should be rather than producing strategies for managing our reality better.
9 Personalisation: blaming ourselves/taking responsibility/feeling guilty for things beyond our control.
10 Labelling and Mis-labelling: applying false/harsh/inappropriate labels to ourselves and/or others.

By helping clients reflect on thinking patterns, explaining the reasons for them and ultimately challenging them, the approach is psycho-educational, problem-oriented and solution-focused.

Cognitive approaches have continued to evolve and from the 1980s Mindfulness-Based Cognitive Therapy has developed. It was founded by Z. Segal, M. Williams and J. Teasdale, who integrated it with an earlier programme designed by J. Kabat-Zinn called Mindfulness-Based Stress Reduction. This off-shoot approach combines Cognitive Therapy, meditation and a cultivation of a present-oriented, non-judgemental attitude called *mindfulness*. It builds on Cognitive Therapy principles by using techniques such as mindfulness meditation, teaching clients to consciously pay attention to thoughts, emotions and feelings without judging them, getting caught up in what could have been or what might be in the future. It's meant to provide clarity of thought, giving clients the capability needed to more easily let go of negative thinking instead of letting them feed depression and anxiety, and relapsing into old negative patterns.

By helping someone alter faulty thinking, we are of course involved in behavioural change of a cognitive nature. Therefore, the approach implicitly includes a strong behavioural dimension. From this, it's easy to understand how the Cognitive and Behavioural methodologies have become closely interlinked to produce Cognitive Behavioural Therapy (CBT), and why Beck is such an influential figure.

So, the key premise is that an individual's experience and evaluation of an event dictates their emotions, feelings and behaviours. If the experience and evaluation (a cognitive process) are negative, then self-defeating thoughts can build in a young developing human, and problems arise.

The *ABC format* developed by Albert Ellis (1960s onwards) is a straightforward way of conceptualising and remembering this last point (see chapters on Cognitive Behaviour Therapy and Rational Emotive Behaviour Therapy):

A: activating event (which is a perceived negative experience).
B: beliefs about the event (automatic/self-defeating thoughts).
C: emotional consequences (which have negative behavioural and physiological responses).

Some Big Names

Beck, J.S. (born 1954): Beck's daughter; a cognitive theoretician and researcher; writer on cognitive therapy treatment and training; co-founder of the Beck Institute for Cognitive Therapy and Research (1994).

Burns, D.D. (1980s onwards): American medical doctor and psychiatrist; student of A. Beck; significant in the sphere of depression; he proposed the theory of *cognitive distortions*.

Kelly, G. (1905–1967): American psychologist, therapist and educator; he developed Personal Construct Theory, a psychological theory of human cognition, prior to Beck's work; said people are *scientists,* and we develop ideas from our life experiences then test them out by acting on them.

Seligman, M.E.P. (born 1942): he worked on positive psychology and developed the concept and theory of *learned helplessness;* inspired by Beck.

Some Big Ideas

Cognitive bias; cognitive shifting; focus of attention; selective abstraction; arbitrary inference; belief testing; negative triads; case formulation; stoicism; homework; client record diary; structured sessions.

How it Works

The goal is to help the client view and evaluate negative thought patterns, and produce ways to replace them with more constructive thinking so forming the basis for change and progress. Practitioner and client come together in a collaborative venture to improve the client's psychological health and well-being, using a systematic application of cognitive and behavioural techniques, the practitioner acting as 'coach' on occasions.

The therapeutic process basically operates in the following way: the practitioner establishes rapport with the client, from which a working alliance develops. In this first phase (say, two sessions) a problem-assessment is conducted and a case formulation/conceptualisation is produced, which then guides the path of the work.

At this point the Cognitive Therapy model can be introduced and psycho-education kicks in, with explanations of such as anxiety, schemas, cognitive distortions and faulty thinking patterns, ABC format and the rationale for a structured approach to each session. From this the anxious client can begin to self-reflect and understand themselves better, knowing that they don't need to worry about 'surprises' popping up in sessions.

Following this, a programme of techniques, exercises and homework is activated so adaptive skills can be created and practised to reduce psychological distress. Also, via testing out automatic thoughts, assessing the evidence (or lack of it) for them, the client is in a position to modify thinking for better functioning, i.e., they become their own scientist.

Termination of the work is in the forefront of the practitioner's mind from the outset, and since Cognitive Therapy is often a short-term intervention (say, 12 sessions, though it usually varies between six and 20 sessions) it's important the adaptive-skills training is well focused and consideration of progress maintenance and relapse prevention is prioritised.

 A brief example

(Using 12 sessions in this case.)
A new client suffers from anxiety, which affects all areas of their life (late 20s, single, employed full-time, shares a flat with a friend): 'I'm a bit of a worrier.' They want to feel more at ease with themselves and 'not get so stressed about everything'.

Initially, you listen and learn about the client, showing respect and empathy, building a constructive relationship with this nervy individual. It's important not to rush them, but the aim is to quickly produce some concrete objectives and have an overall stated goal for the counselling. To reduce any session-anxiety in the client, you explain straightforwardly the Cognitive Therapy approach and concepts, giving reasons for sessions being structured, plus the importance of homework. Also, this is when you explain and clarify anything the client needs to know about anxiety and its effects.

Suppose you both agree to commence with the client learning about the ABC format, which involves keeping a diary of anxiety-provoking events and consequences, and aids them to know their patterns of *cognitive distortions*. You both agree to focus on client confidence-issues at work, which also overlaps with friendship relationships.

At the start of each session check over homework and decide between you what will be the focus this time, remembering that you might be called upon to take on the role of a *motivational coach* – but that doesn't give you the right to be critical, judgemental or directive! This sets a base for the client to ponder and understand their previous thought and behaviour patterns, check the evidence for them (reviewing their negative *schemas* and *belief systems*), see the faulty thinking, and so recognise the logic for appropriate change. If you do this, a safe and positive working environment can be created, with the client *scientist* practising new ways of being, gathering supportive weekly evidence via homework and self-rating pro forma during sessions, which allows for anxiety levels to decrease.

Over the following weeks the client explores, ponders and understands where their anxieties stem from via *cognitive homework* exercises about their relationships with 'adult' figures. For example, they realise their uncertainty around powerful authority figures comes from having an 'all-knowing' parent who tried to protect the client from the vagaries of life at the expense of the client learning to find their own way through difficulties and learning to stand on their own two feet, so to speak. The client sees how a well-meaning significant adult unintentionally restricted competence and confidence development in the child. This includes reviewing client *cognitive distortions*, such as jumping to negative conclusions about how they will be judged if they ask to take a full lunch-hour to visit the dentist (their work attendance is excellent) or

(Continued)

49

(Continued)

how friends will be annoyed if the client declines to go to a party, 'If I don't go, they won't invite me to the next one...'.

From gaining this insight, the client is less self-critical and has a greater comprehension of how they came to be as they were when they entered the counselling process. They acknowledge it took some courage to arrive and face their issues, and they start to think positively about themselves. By the time the 12 sessions are completed the client is less anxious and more self-appreciative, feeling able to face others and life due to a new perspective on who they are and how they can be with others.

Who it's For

Evidence suggests the approach is effective for such as (adolescent) depression; anxiety; OCD; bipolar disorder; sexual dysfunction; eating disorders; Post Traumatic Stress Disorder; substance misuse; (borderline) personality disorders; schizophrenia; repeat-attempts suicide clients; sleeping problems; Asperger's Syndrome. It's extensively used in the mental health and educational spheres.

It's suggested Cognitive Therapy is suitable for children, adolescents and adults.

Critical Considerations

Substantial research has been conducted into this approach, particularly with regard to depression and anxiety, with supportive conclusions; it can be used in the short term with relatively quick results; it can be less 'scary' than some other methods, apparently.

On the other hand, critics argue that it doesn't always go deep enough; it doesn't necessarily fit with clients who like to be/benefit from being challenged; the practitioner can fall into the 'lead' role and/or be directive rather than simply being a coach.

The approach may not benefit clients who seek to explore their past in depth as the focus is mainly in the here-and-now.

Identifying Features

Usually a short-term approach; psycho-educational; utilised with some of the more serious 'mental health' conditions; progress maintenance/relapse prevention is a priority; a focus on endings; firm foundation-stone of the CBT approach.

Reflections

I believe Cognitive Therapy, its rationale and ideas are straightforward for students to learn. It logically and clearly links cognitions, emotions, feelings and behaviours. The 10 common faulty-thinking patterns resonate with me personally, socially and professionally, and are useful guides when listening to others in my attempts to understand them (and myself!). Similarly, the ABC format is a useful reference point for students and practitioners when reflecting on this approach as it's an easy concept to understand when considering the way people are and how they respond to situations. Also, once clients have integrated the format, many use it to monitor themselves as part of the change process, in my experience.

The importance of the information-giving and psycho-education dimension is something for students to take seriously. It indicates there's more to being a practitioner than simply learning the theory of your chosen approach and developing your communication skills. Being well informed about a wide variety of psychological issues is, indeed, a challenge, but is increasingly necessary in our work.

My final point in this section relates to the title of the approach; for me, Cognitive Therapy, with its significant behavioural component, e.g., thinking and action-based homework, exercises, and change, is clearly a cognitive behavioural methodology, one of the first of its kind. Yet, the behavioural dimension isn't formally acknowledged in the name. I think, therefore, that the approach is too narrow in its description of itself. By not formally including this crucial dimension, perhaps Cognitive Therapy does itself a slight disservice?

Relating to this is the focus of Beck and his colleagues since the 1980s; from that period he has increasingly referred to, and taught courses in, Cognitive Behaviour Therapy. Therefore we have something else to reflect on – has the time of Cognitive Therapy in its own right come and gone...?

Summary

Cognitive Therapy is a structured, educational, generally short-term approach to assisting clients to reduce psychological distress and dysfunction by changing negative thought patterns, and so improving future functioning. It has a strong evidence base and is employed in the mental health sphere particularly, though it transfers well to other areas, being applicable to people of all ages. It's a foundation of the hybrid Cognitive Behavioural Approach.

Learning Ideas

1 Think about how a Cognitive Therapist might help a male client experiencing sexual dysfunction in the form of premature ejaculation, and write your ideas down on some A4 paper.

2 Reflect on yourself, and consider this question deeply: How often do I jump to conclusions, and why?

3 Revision

a Make sure you know the 10 common patterns of cognitive distortion.

b Consider how a practitioner might move from being a 'coach' to the 'leader' during sessions, and how they can prevent this from happening.

c Learn about anxiety and depression as they are common conditions and you are training to be an educator as a dimension of your work.

Suggested Reading

Beck, J.S. (1995) *Cognitive Therapy: Basics and Beyond*. New York: Guilford Press.

Free, M.L. (2007) *Cognitive Therapy in Groups: Guidelines for Practice* (2nd edition). Chichester: Wiley.

Turkington, D. et al. (2009) *Back to Life, Back to Normality: Cognitive Therapy, Recovery and Psychosis*. Cambridge: Cambridge University Press.

6

Developmental Counselling

Origins and Background

Gerard Egan, an American psychologist (1950s onwards), was interested in educating clients about self-development via counselling so they could understand themselves more and produce improved ways to manage their lives. While he saw people as active, adaptable and capable of development, he also said we have a 'bottomless pit' of self-inhibiting, negative processes he later referred to as our *shadow side*. Egan's view of people was that we behave according to how we perceive a given situation (e.g., if you feel worried and think counselling practice will be difficult, it probably will be!). His early focus included the skills needed for family life, initial parenting, lifestyle management, career development and interpersonal relationships.

He introduced his Developmental Approach, which derives from Rogerian roots (please see Chapter 10 on Person-Centred Counselling), to the world in 1975. It also takes strongly from cognitive and behavioural schools of thought, and has recently been described as a person-centred cognitive behavioural approach (Palmer, 2000).

Other areas that played into Egan's thinking were counselling-skills training approaches, *social influence theory* (basically, this is when we are affected by other people, and it can take various forms, e.g., conformity, peer pressure, obedience, sales and marketing, leadership) and *learning theory* (essentially, we learn to behave in situations according to experiences from similar earlier events and our thoughts about them).

Egan initially said Developmental Counselling was a practical approach, then later, an integrating framework for *doing* therapeutic work.

He believed a practitioner needs to develop high levels of competence and sensitivity in their efforts to become a *skilled helper*, focusing much on this aspect of the counsellor–client relationship. Further, he said the role of the practitioner can involve information-giving and psycho-education so clients can learn about their development and competencies in order to improve future functioning. This implies students of the Developmental Approach should be well grounded in the major schools of thought mentioned at the start of this book.

Therefore, education and skills development of the client *and* the (student) practitioner are key ideas in Egan's perspective, which has two main aims:

1 Assisting clients to manage problems in living more effectively and developing underlying resources and opportunities.
2 Aiding clients to become more functional as self-managers in their lives.

The approach was first described as a problem-solving, then problem-management methodology, and now many of Egan's followers take a more solution-focused standpoint with a greater emphasis on the future. This fits well with his view that, while appreciating our roots and how they affect us, the past should not be the major focus of the client's self-exploration work.

The original model had three stages but in the 1990s it was tinkered with and some added a fourth, basically by splitting Stage 3 into two parts. In fact, it has evolved

55

regularly over the years, with Egan updating his famous book, *The Skilled Helper* on a number of occasions. That said, many practitioners continue to work within the original framework.

More recently Egan talked about *principles of practice* and an *integrating framework* rather than guidelines or rules. He has also worked on a people-in-systems model where practitioners need knowledge of both human life-span developmental processes and *life skills* for clients to succeed with developmental tasks.

The Developmental Approach continues to be used by many and is the predecessor of the Integrative Approach in the UK which came to prominence in the 1990s.

▬▬▬ Some Big Names ▬▬▬

Carkhuff, R. (1930s–1940s onwards): clinical psychologist; into skills-training; he was a leading player in putting theory into practice regarding counselling and human development; an early colleague of Carl Rogers.

Erikson, E. (1940s onwards; died in 1994): American developmental psychologist and psychoanalyst; produced an eight-stage theory of social development, and in each stage a person meets and hopefully overcomes new challenges; he was interested in the psychology of personal identity and coined the phrase *identity crisis*; studied Montessori Education, which has a focus on child development.

Gilmore, S. (1940s onwards): she was an American psychologist into counsellor training; clinical work; research; organisational development; educational development.

Kennedy, E. (born 1928; significant from 1960s): American clinical psychologist; ex-priest; radical Roman Catholic; into the psychology of the priesthood; wrote about the requisites for becoming a counsellor.

Some Big Ideas

Skills-based; developmental map; core concepts; client responsibility; contracts; the shadow side; integrative versus eclectic; SOLER; SMART goals; human ecology.

How it Works

Establishing a strong therapeutic relationship is crucial, as it is with other approaches, and Egan suggested certain core concepts are the foundation of a sound counsellor–client dynamic:

- Empathy (cognitive and emotional understanding).
- Respect (relates to positive regard, acceptance and a non-judgemental attitude).
- Genuineness (relates to congruence).

The aim is for the client and practitioner to explore the origins and effects of the issue(s) so they both come to a point of greater understanding of what they are dealing with, and then actively work on a strategy for change.

Within this, the Developmental Approach asks clients three core questions:

1 Where are you now?
2 Where do you want to get to?
3 How can you get there?

Flexibility is needed in applying the approach since clients might have a number of issues, and be at different stages with each of them.

The three-stage version is as follows:

Stage 1: exploring, identifying and clarifying issues and unused opportunities.
Stage 2: broadening client perspectives and developing a preferred scenario.
Stage 3: action, review and evaluation of action taken.

Stage 1 is particularly important: it's about the exploration and understanding of the client by the practitioner, and the understanding of the client by the client. With increased understanding of what they are dealing with, both parties are likelier to jointly formulate more feasible outcomes for lasting constructive change.

So, Stage 1 explores issues and is basically person-centred. Exploring emotions means thinking about them and links to Stage 2 which is cognitive, where actions and behaviours to improve client functioning are considered. This then leads on to Stage 3, which is behavioural (action-based) and incorporates SMART goal-setting.

 A brief example

A new client suffers from anxiety, which affects all areas of their life (late 20s, single, employed full-time, shares a flat with a friend): 'I'm a bit of a worrier'. They want to feel more at ease with themselves and 'not get so stressed out about everything'.

First, an important focus for you is establishing a strong therapeutic relationship, building rapport, trust and a collaborative approach about the work to come, leading to setting clear goals, so it shouldn't be rushed. This is where the core concepts need to be

Developmental Counselling

implemented via sensitive use of appropriate verbal interventions and non-verbal activity. Do this by using communication skills such as reflecting emotions, paraphrasing, clarifying, open questions, concrete examples, active listening skills, using para-language (e.g., 'mmh', 'aah', 'yeah'), non-verbal communication, silences (don't be scared of them; they can be your friend – they allow you to observe and monitor the client, collect your thoughts, and train you not to speak unnecessarily! It also gives the client thinking time), summarising, which is also a standard way of finishing a session.

Bear in mind that some anxious people don't trust easily whereas others will want to put themselves entirely in your hands. In either case, trust and honesty are imperative here, which includes owning the limitations of yourself, i.e., ultimately, the client will get out what they put in, in terms of successful change, and your role is to help them help themselves. Be clear and up-front about this.

From there both parties think about how to move towards change for better functioning. The client may be 'stuck' about being able to go forward (anxiety can relate to low self-esteem and a lack of confidence) and that's where skills like *challenge* come in – but remember we can challenge people about the positive things they have, which can assist progress. Don't automatically consider challenging as a negative – it's not. Also remember this important point: you have to earn the right to challenge, so be sure the therapeutic relationship is well established and stable before you jump in. Sensitivity is vital.

An agreed strategy, possibly including homework, can be produced; one way is to rank topics for improvement and decide which one to work on first. Often it's the least threatening, in order to increase confidence levels and a belief that change is achievable.

Perhaps, as a starting point, the client opts for relaxation and breathing exercises to help reduce overall anxiety levels. This requires focused thinking and practice to blot out negative thoughts while doing the exercise. Thus, the practitioner is involved in educating the client to cope better in their environment but the responsibility is with the client as to how much

(Continued)

59

(Continued)

effort will be put into the process, which obviously relates to how successful it will be.

Next, the plan is implemented. The client reports session-by-session on progress, with you monitoring and evaluating the work in relation to the stated desired outcomes agreed earlier in the relationship. The idea is that if the client makes sufficient progress they will have the confidence and motivation to tackle the next item on their ranking list, while becoming more responsible for themselves.

Each stage is fluidly linked to the following one. Finally, remember *evaluation* is very important, and is best conducted on a session-by-session basis.

As progress is made with individual items the client becomes more independent of you and a better self-manager, reaching a point where they confidently arrive at sessions with ideas for problem-management without having to run them by you first.

Who's it For

It has widespread usage, e.g., education (students, staff, parent-figures); family services; offending; substances work; mental health; organisational development (individuals, staff groups, managers); careers counselling.

The Developmental Approach can be used with children, young people and adults (including group-work).

Critical Considerations

This methodology might be described as a *theoretical integrative* approach, incorporating much from the person-centred philosophy and approach plus cognitive and behavioural features in a rational manner. Another way to describe it could be as a *systematic* or *structured* integrative method.

Skills-appropriateness derives from studies conducted by such as Carl Rogers; skills-based for what is, after all, an applied discipline.

There is general supportive evidence for generic problem-solving/solution-focused modalities, of which the Developmental Approach is one.

It's adaptable to multiple therapeutic and other contexts.

Globally, it continues to be the most widely taught approach on counselling training programmes, which could be viewed as supportive empirical evidence for its efficacy.

The approach has been criticised for being too structured and not flexible enough, and while nodding towards the use of psychodynamic concepts, it doesn't formally integrate this major school of thought.

Identifying Features

Structured yet flexible; incorporates person-centred, cognitive and behavioural concepts; emphasises the practitioner as both educator and learner; takes into account the interactions between clients and their physical and social environments (human ecology).

Reflections

Though designed for long-term work, the Developmental Approach adapts to a shorter version (say, 16 sessions, including an initial assessment and a final progress review meeting). It stresses practitioner competencies, students learning that certain communication techniques are more appropriately used in different stages (e.g., open questions are preferable to closed ones in Stage 1) and they study the rationale for a particular skill's use.

Remember that while the practitioner may be an information-giver and educator, their role is not about giving guidance or advice; the responsibility for change lies with the client and the decisions and effort they make. It's important for you to bear this in mind as you go through your training.

Egan refers to four stages of learning for students, which they experience to become effective practitioners and which can be passed on to 'learners' they work with:

1 Unconscious incompetence (getting it wrong, and not realising it…!).
2 Conscious incompetence (getting it wrong, and realising it – can be embarrassing, but stay with it).
3 Conscious competence (getting it right, and knowing it – practical progress).
4 Unconscious competence (getting it right without thinking about it – skills are now integrating into your counselling work).

He said that helper levels of communication skills and personal qualities are vital in using the approach sensitively and flexibly as we attempt to empower people to function better.

On a personal note, I find the Developmental Approach to be a solid foundation for counselling in sport settings with talented/elite athletes (individuals, teams, squads) to develop their performance levels in sporting competitions (e.g., British, Commonwealth, European, World, Olympic Games), and conflict resolution or mediation work.

Summary

The Developmental Approach is a structured yet fluid integrative method, person-centred and cognitive-behavioural at its core. It's useful for both short-term and long-term work, adaptable to various settings, and used with a range of age groups. It's concerned with practitioners developing skills and abilities to utilise at the most appropriate times to help people to be improved self-managers. It takes seriously interactions between clients and their physical and social psychological environments, perhaps more than some other approaches.

Learning Ideas

1   Draw a 'road-map' of your life, focusing on major moments. Don't use words on the paper. Then ponder what you've drawn and why. Put your drawing into words on A4 paper. Next, imagine someone reading what you've written. How does that make you feel and think?
2   What's in your personal *shadow side*, and what are you doing about it? Remember, self-awareness and development significantly depend on your self-honesty, especially if you want to be a quality practitioner.
3   Revision

    a   Consider *integrative* and *eclectic* and make sure you know the differences between them.
    b   Think about how to prevent an integrative practitioner from being a 'bits and pieces' worker who simply muddles through.
    c   Reflect on the benefits and limitations of using a structured integrative counselling approach.

 **Suggested Reading**

Blocher, D.H. (2000) *Counselling: A Developmental Approach* (4th edition). Chichester: Wiley.

Egan, G. (2004) *The Skilled Helper.* Pacific Grove, CA: Wadsworth.

Ivey, A.E., Ivey, M.B., Myers, J.E. and Sweeney, T.J. (2004) *Developmental Counselling & Therapy: Promoting Wellness over the Lifespan.* Boston, MA: Houghton-Mifflin.

7

Existential Counselling

Origins and Background

The approach derives from existential philosophy and phenomenology.

It could be suggested that the person having the biggest initial influence on the development of this approach was Martin Heidegger (1889–1976), considered by many as the founder of Existentialism. His philosophy impacted on Swiss psychiatrists M. Boss (1903–1990) and L. Binswanger (1881–1966), who utilised it in their psychotherapy which could be called the start of the Existential counselling approach.

Many significant figures abound in this philosophy, including S.A. Kierkegaard (1813–1855), a Danish philosopher who highlighted the importance of personal choice and commitment when living our lives. His psychological work explored emotions and feelings about our life choices. Another was German philosopher and philologist F.W. Nietzsche (1844–1900), who believed people should challenge the constraints of given morality and society, and discover their free will. Some of his major themes were freedom, responsibility, choice and courage. J.-P. Sartre (1905–1980), an influential French existential philosopher wanted individuals to live *authentically*, dealing with life's experiences as they appear and not depending on a knowledge-base or others for our survival.

E.G.A. Husserl (1859–1938) was the philosopher credited with founding phenomenology, the study of conscious experience, e.g., emotions, perception, thinking, judgements, which related to the thinking and work of the philosophers just mentioned.

In the UK, leading Existentialist theorists and practitioners included Scottish psychiatrist R.D. Laing (1927–1989), who took Sartre's existential ideas as the basis for his own work, and D. Cooper (1931–1986), a South African psychiatrist and leader of the anti-psychiatry movement. They collaborated on reviewing the notion of mental illness and its treatment, believing madness and psychosis are symptoms of dysfunction between an individual's *true* identity and their social identity (given by others, which are then internalised).

Another way to consider psychological health is to view it as a capacity to deal with life's complications, the world and relationships within it. *Disturbance* occurs as the result of avoiding life's truths and living according to other people's demands and expectations. While disturbances are inevitable, the question is how we respond to them – openly and assertively taking on the challenges, anxieties and all, or withdrawing, giving in and taking no responsibility for ourselves, our decisions and their consequences (remember, *not* making a decision is in itself a decision!).

Gradually, Existential therapeutic approaches arrived. They included some general concepts from the core philosophical thinking espoused by such as the individuals mentioned above, plus many others.

Existential counselling sees people as creatures of continual change and transformation, with personal strengths and weaknesses, and environmental opportunities, challenges

and limitations. This explains why Existential practitioners don't appreciate ideas like personality types, fixed
psychological categories for patients/clients, diagnosis and
formalised treatment regimes.

The approach is about exploring meaning and value,
and learning to live *authentically*, i.e., according to our
own values and priorities, not those planted in us by others. It's about becoming true to ourselves and being honest
about our real possibilities, limitations and fears. It means
living in a self-directed, thoughtful, even courageous way,
rather than being ruled by others and effectively living for
them. That said, the approach focuses more on the client's
present and future than on the past.

Existential therapy operates on the belief that a person's inner conflicts come from their difficulties with the
givens of existence (also known as *ultimate concerns*):

- Death and its inevitability.
- Freedom and responsibility.
- The isolation of personal existence.
- Meaningless/the worth of life.

These are seen as natural and predictable stresses of the
four dimensions of existence:

1 Physical.
2 Social.
3 Personal.
4 Spiritual.

Some other orientations claim to be existential but it can
be argued that to be so a therapy needs to take into
account the cultural, social, political and ideological contexts of a client's existence, and not all methodologies
seem to make this an area of priority or emphasis.

Some Big Names

Frankl, V. (1905–1997): Austrian neurologist and psychiatrist; he developed logotherapy, which says the most powerful human drive is to find meaning for our lives.

May, R. (1909–1994): American existential psychologist; associated with humanistic psychology; he proposed stages of psychological human development.

van Deurzen, E. (born 1951): Dutch, living in the UK; psychotherapist and educator (especially in Existential counselling); she is a significant influence in establishing existential therapy in the UK; ex-Chair of UKCP.

Yalom, I.D. (born 1931): American psychiatrist and psychotherapist; into existential group psychotherapy; developed his own model; worked on the *givens* of existence.

 Some Big Ideas

Existential anxiety; existential guilt; interpreted world; facticity; freedom; being-in-the-world; problems in living; call of conscience; logotherapy; phenomenological reduction; practitioner self-awareness.

How it Works

Existential practitioners say there's no typical session format, since every counselling dynamic varies because people are different from each other, so an individualised approach is taken (this relates to the person-centred approach).

Similarly, there are no set rules for this therapy and Existentialists are taught to develop their own practice style based on the guiding philosophy and principles, which include session agendas being set by the client, equality between the two parties and a trusting, warm, supportive counselling relationship. Through establishing such an environment, the aim is for the client to start exploring their internal rules, attitudes, assumptions about themselves, others, the world, and understand themselves and their inhibiting disturbances. From this they begin to see possibilities for greater personal freedom and choices while taking on more self-responsibility.

Practitioner self-awareness is crucial for competent Existential counselling and vital for self-monitoring in their work. They need to show respect, acceptance and empathy in order to better understand their client's life experience. Particularly useful competences include accurate paraphrasing, open and non-judgemental questions, clarification, summarising, use of silence and non-interpretation.

Further, this approach requires practitioner self-discipline, i.e., they need to approach the counselling process and each session with a completely open mind. This can be a demanding professional requirement for some of us, but it's achievable via hard work on ourselves.

The Existential practitioner facilitates the client's engagement with themselves without imposing their own judgements as this can prevent full understanding and empathy. Instead, practitioners help clients develop their own perspectives rather than living by the pressures, rules, ideas of others (including those of the practitioner!). By achieving this freedom, clients can begin to live in their own ways, meeting the vagaries of existence head on, appreciating this is the way the world operates. They also take responsibility for their actions and consequences without blaming others for the state of their lives.

When working with clients, a practitioner might employ a four-part construction to frame their thinking for the counselling process and understanding of the client:

1   The client's existence regarding the physical world, health and illness.
2   The social dimension of client relationships in the outside world.
3   The psychological or personal dimension of the client, i.e., relationship with themselves and others.
4   The spiritual dimension, which relates to client ideals, philosophy and ultimate meanings.

To underline the point, this construction isn't imposed; it helps form the way in which the practitioner thinks and comprehends the client's world and existence.

 A brief example

A new client suffers from anxiety, which affects all areas of their life (late 20s, single, employed full-time, shares a flat with a friend): 'I'm a bit of a worrier.' They want to feel more at ease with themselves and 'not get so stressed about everything'.

Let's say the client explains why they've come but are unsure quite where to start. You empathise, paraphrase and reflect accurately, allowing them time to begin while conducting an assessment of them. Within this accepting and non-critical atmosphere they slowly commence talking about their present circumstances and immediate issues. You go with their flow, encouraging them to lead you into their frame of reference/view of life, utilising the competences mentioned above. This also shows respect for them and can be validating and empowering.

At one point, the client says they are not used to talking like this; they have a caring, protective parent who has always been strongly present in their life as a mentor and guide, and who is very firm in their attitudes. The client speaks of anxiety about getting things wrong and lacking confidence about making their own decisions, as the parent has '...always been there for me, pointing me in the right direction'. They don't want to be a disappointment in the eyes of their parent and significant others (e.g., friends, line managers, employers). Therefore, the sessions are stressful for them as you aren't deciding what to work on and you don't guide, advise or instruct.

Nevertheless, the client perseveres and over time they relate their anxiety, erratic confidence and uncertainty in decision-making to ideas and rules socialised into them by others as they grew. This includes not wanting to let down their parent and manager and end up being criticised for getting something wrong. You work to stay with them, listening carefully, seeking clarification of their emotions, thoughts and behaviours as they become accustomed to examining their inner self, and how they have come to be as they are now. Remember, intervene, but don't interrupt.

Work continues at the client's pace, with them setting the agenda and deciding the focus for each session. You listen carefully, evidencing an attitude that is supportive, encouraging and non-judgemental, as the client reassesses the influences on their life. They explore how they have come to be affected by unintended inhibiting disturbances from significant people, and by extension, authority figures and confident individuals. They have greater self-awareness now.

Over time the client opens up about their historical way of *being-in-the-world*, exploring and reaching understanding of their anxiety issues. They move on to deciding to live more *authentically,* dealing with the existential guilt of becoming their own person at the expense of their parent and others, and the continuing but manageable anxieties of life. The client is moving towards enhanced confidence at handling the freedom they have finally grasped.

Some of you might worry at the prospect of not having a set format for the work or fixed agenda for sessions – there's no need for that if you keep the clear guiding principles of Existential counselling in mind. Also, you can start each session with a summary of what happened last time and finish with another relating to the work carried out on this occasion, which helps with a sense of order as well as constituting good practice.

Who it's For

The approach appears appropriate for people who see their issues as challenges of living; are genuinely interested in self-awareness and self-exploration; have an interest in the search for meaning in their lives; are at the edge of existence, i.e., contemplating suicide.

For some clients it might seem too unstructured an approach. However, supporters argue that Existential counselling, at least theoretically, is useful to anyone because it focuses on the particular individual, working closely with their personal perspectives and experience.

It probably isn't a very suitable approach for children.

Critical Considerations

The general approach has been accused of being nihilistic and pessimistic, though many Existentialists argue this is an unfair interpretation since they actually take an optimistic stance on people's potential for managing the anxieties of life.

The Existential approach has been criticised for 'intellectualising' client life situations, though this in turn has been refuted for misinterpretation of simply discovering how a person perceives and lives in the world.

Some might consider the approach has a rather narrow appeal, being more suitable for people prepared to explore and re-evaluate their place in the world and not for those who want more immediate resolution of issues. This infers a longer-term counselling process for participants.

There isn't much research evidence yet for the potency of Existential Therapy.

Identifying Features

Practitioners develop their own style, adapting to each client; non-directive and client-led; unstructured; based in philosophy; longer-term generally, though some use it in short-term work.

Reflections

Existential counselling is about the practitioner having an attitude based on a world view of how to face and live life which forms the core of their therapeutic work and own way of living. In many respects this resonates with the Person-Centred Approach and principles of practitioner-living. Such a view isn't comfortable for all students and practitioners because some of us 'put on our counselling hat' for the work but our personal ways of dealing with life may not dove-tail with our practice and therapeutic principles. So, Existentialism doesn't appeal to all.

Similarly, others prefer more structured approaches and might be drawn to different modalities.

Existential therapy is reality-based and up-front about the nature of our world, i.e., full of anxieties, demands, pressures and stresses.

I appreciate the broad sweep that Existential counselling has, i.e., it explores the way everything we do is dependent on our life contexts, assisting clients to clarify and understand their world view, values, beliefs and making internal client operations become explicit.

I see similarities with the philosophies of the Person-Centred Approach and Gestalt Therapy.

============ **Summary** ============

The Existential approach derives from existential philosophy and phenomenology, being concerned with how clients deal with the issues of living. It's essentially person-centred, the practitioner perceiving each client as unique and adapting their therapeutic style to every individual they work with. Theoretically, it's applicable to everyone, but in practice its unstructured nature doesn't fit all practitioners and clients. It aims to help people see the inhibiting factors in their lives, reconsider perspectives, take responsibility and live more freely in the face of the challenges and anxieties of existence. It's a longer-term approach.

============ **Learning Ideas** ============

1 View your developing individual style in relation to Existential principles, owning any difficulties you might have. Write this down to clarify where you are with your counselling knowledge, methodological preferences and developing approach.

2 Ponder the concept of death – what physical feelings, emotions and thoughts do you experience, and why?

3 Revision

a Make sure you understand how logotherapy works.

b Be clear about why Existentialists don't believe that full psychological health is possible.

c Check that you know these meanings: authenticity; with-world; call of conscience; being condemned to choose; disturbances; facticity; phenomenological reduction.

 **Suggested Reading**

Barnett, L. (2009) *When Death Enters the Therapeutic Space: Existential Perspectives in Psychotherapy & Counselling.* Hove: Routledge.

Cooper, M. (2003) *Existential Therapies.* London: Sage.

van Deurzen, E. and Adams, M. (2011) *Skills in Existential Counselling & Psychotherapy.* London: Sage.

8

Gestalt Therapy

================ **Origins and Background** ================

Fritz Perls (1893–1970), a German psychiatrist and psychotherapist living in America, working with his wife Laura, developed Gestalt Therapy (1940s onwards).

This approach is based on Gestalt Psychology (Gestaltism) and Gestalt Theory, which appeared in the early years of the 20th century; they state that the operating principle of Gestalt is that the brain is holistic, i.e., like a system, as in people. It can't be explained by component parts alone; rather the system as a whole mainly determines how the parts behave.

The word *Gestalt* is German, meaning the *essence* of an entity's complete form. In English, we understand the term via the ancient Greek philosopher Aristotle: 'The whole is greater than the sum of its parts.'

The original therapy is known as *classical* Gestalt, which focused on developing client general self-awareness.

Contemporary Gestalt focuses more on the concept of *contact*, i.e., awareness of our relationship with ourselves, others and the world. In current practice and theory, the therapeutic relationship is a major interest area of this contact idea. Within this, discussing the differences in how the practitioner and client view the processes and dynamics between them leads to further dialogue (this led to the development of Dialogical Psychotherapy) and the process progresses. The two parties concentrate on their respective immediate sensory and perceptual experience, these factors being considered the most important in the counselling work and the client's general life. This constitutes the *phenomenological* foundation of the therapy. Gestaltists believe a client's subjective experience is more important and reliable to work with than interpretations and explanations (which can lead both away from the *here-and-now* feelings they experience and can be focused on intellectual and emotional discussions about the past, etc.) which in turn relates to underlying client emotions and ways of being. Thus, client awareness development leading to realisation and understanding is viewed as more powerful than practitioner clinical diagnosis and direction.

Later, Erving and Miriam Polster proposed a second theoretical emphasis, the contact between one person (self) and another, and ultimately the *dialogical* relationship between practitioner and client.

Alongside the dialogical relationship idea, *field theory* arrived: a person's *field* incorporates two dimensions:

1 Ontology: the philosophical study of *being, existence* or *reality*.
2 Phenomenology: the physical and environmental contexts in which a person exists.

The American Dick Price more recently developed Gestalt Practice (1980s), which is presented as a form of personal exploration and method of awareness techniques rather than therapy. It's most often taught in groups. An off-shoot of this is Gestalt Awareness Practice, led by Christine Stewart Price, Dick's wife, and quite popular in the USA.

Gestalt Therapy has been described in numerous ways:

- An existential, experiential and humanistic approach emphasising personal responsibility. Existentialism states that we have responsibility for our own lives, choices and decisions, the primary emphasis being on increasing personal awareness of being in the world. Humanism stresses our inborn capacity for constructive development and change.
- A process-oriented therapy because it's more concerned with what's happening in the session right now (process), not with what's being discussed (content).
- A holistic approach taking account of mind, body, background and culture.
- Multi-systemic because it sees the complications of people living in complex situations.
- A method of awareness practice which some other approaches call *mindfulness*. Clients learn to be more self-aware of what they're doing, how they're being and what they're feeling physically (in relation to their environment and interpersonal dynamics with others). From this, understanding develops, leading to the ability to take risks and make changes.

So, Gestalt Therapy has cognitive elements because clients have to consider meanings of the way they feel, and why, plus how to deal with their emotions, negative thinking and actions. The focus is on what is being felt, thought, done in the present moment rather than on what was, might be, could be or should have been.

The aim of Gestalt counselling is to help people free themselves from *blocks* and *unfinished business* which inhibit personal growth, so it's considered a humanistic approach.

Some Big Names

Goldstein, K. (1878–1965): German neurologist and psychiatrist; he developed a holistic model of the human organism based on Gestalt theory, which influenced Gestalt Therapy development.

Goodman, P. (1911–1972): American sociologist; he was one of the founders of Gestalt theory and Gestalt Therapy.

Hefferline, R.F. (1910–1974): American psychologist; former patient of Perls; he became a co-worker in developing Gestalt Therapy.

Perls, L. (1905–1990): German wife of Perls; psychologist and psychotherapist; initially influenced by Sigmund Freud's psycho-analysis; she helped develop Gestalt from its inception.

Some Big Ideas

Empty chair technique; unfinished business; process-oriented not content-focused; introjections ('shoulds', 'oughts', 'musts'); creative adjustment; interruptions to contact (e.g., projection, retroflection, confluence; deflection); dream-work; being in the present; client self-responsibility.

How it Works

The aim is to enable clients to become free of inhibiting blocks and unfinished business so they can grow and fulfil their potential as their own person. Awareness experiments and training are vital to self-development so form an important base for the counselling work. The creation of a strong, trusting therapeutic relationship is crucial. The practitioner focuses on the *what* and *how* of what the client brings with less concern on the *why*.

The counselling process has three components the client needs to consider:

1   How they historically and currently respond (*creative adjustment*).

2   What factors make them respond in the way they do in the present.
3   They can decide to change (*self-responsibility*).

Gestalt states that change occurs when a client strives to be who they truly are instead of staying as someone they're not. This can be achieved within a supportive, trusting relationship without pressure or judgemental-ism from the practitioner. By becoming more aware of what's negatively impacting on the client, and how, they are in a better position to ponder the understanding of that person. If the practitioner works empathically and respectfully with the client's present experience and feelings, they can engender an appropriate atmosphere for change. Thus, a client is assisted to feel their *here-and-now* and experiment with experiences which might help their self-awareness to increase and reduce blocks to awareness and change in their lives, including *unfinished business*.

The next statement may seem strange, even scary, to some of you, while others may find it interesting or even exciting – it's not really possible to describe a typical Gestalt session because there isn't one! There's no fixed format. Sessions are based on whatever the client brings. The practitioner's sensitivity, creativity and spontaneous thinking are their focus and key tools, not a session agenda with a set direction and concrete outcome.

The straightforward aim is to enhance the client's self-awareness leading to change.

Within the process, differences in perspectives between practitioner and client become the experimental focus, as does *dialogue* (communicating phenomenological viewpoints), i.e., engaging clients in interpersonal dialogue to address issues and not directing them towards a clinical goal.

A brief example

(This example utilises a contemporary approach.)
A new client suffers from anxiety, which affects all areas of their life (late 20s, single, employed full-time, shares a flat with a friend): 'I'm a bit of a worrier.' They want to feel more at ease with themselves and 'not get so stressed about everything'.

First, you conduct a client assessment, including personal details, remembering to explain and stress that it's the client who decides what the agenda will be for each session.

Simultaneously, carefully observe the client and tell them how Gestalt works.

Perhaps you start gently, asking how the client feels in their first session with you. It's worth noting here that some people lack physical self-awareness or may be instantly uncertain talking about themselves, which is why your ability to establish a non-threatening environment is vital from the start. Let's say the client answers your enquiries as best they can; that should give you some idea as to what you're dealing with. You encourage the client to feel this early anxiety of being in a room with a stranger who they see as a cross between an authority figure and an inquisitor, inviting them to talk about the physical sensations they experience.

Gradually, as you build rapport with them, the client begins to talk about what might lie behind their anxiety and how they have perceived you. It turns out they have a caring parent who historically 'knows best' how to keep their child safe from the risks of life, giving advice, guidance, instruction about how the person should be, which the client has adapted to as they grew (*creative adjustment*). Over forthcoming meetings the client talks negatively about

(Continued)

(Continued)

authority figures, stemming from the physical sensations they feel when they speak about such people specifically and generally. They fret about being criticised by these individuals.

The client learns the association between feeling anxious, disloyal, frustrated, resentful, and the low confidence they have as they explore their 'lack of opportunity to think for myself, and why I'm not sure about making my own decisions now I'm grown up' (*interruptions to contact*). However, as the process proceeds in the supportive and empowering therapeutic dynamic with you, the client's physical tension levels decrease. They speak more easily about the parent in the third person in this experiential experimental environment, beginning to assert themselves more as they wish to be rather than who they have learned to be.

At an appropriate moment, with confidence levels higher, the client practises speaking to the parent in the first person, directing their words to an *empty chair*. Progress continues in this way until the client fulfils their potential by becoming the person they truly are, accepting and integrating a belief in the concept of *self-responsibility*. They claim the right to make their own decisions as an adult, now free of the anxieties associated with being judged poorly or led by others.

Who it's For

Gestaltists are trained to undertake work guided by their levels of qualification, knowledge and experience, so some may counsel people with deep anxiety, anger or depression, for example, while other practitioners don't for reasons just mentioned.

That said, the approach is applicable to a wide range of issues and clients of different ages, e.g., organisational development work, personal coaching, teaching (including with younger people). Numerous ideas have been incorporated into other therapeutic modalities.

Traditionally, Gestalt has been considered most effective with anxious, phobic, depressed and perfectionist clients.

Critical Considerations

As cognitive approaches became influential from the 1970s, Gestalt was viewed as something of an anachronism, losing a lot of popularity.

At that time many Gestaltists reacted adversely to the drive for research into therapy and they ignored such work, which didn't help the development of Gestalt theory and practice. However, around the turn of the 21st century attitudes began to shift and more research now takes place.

While techniques have been borrowed by other approaches, this has sometimes brought unwarranted criticism of Gestalt because some practitioners have used techniques out of context, so seeming to miss overall understanding of the rationale for their usage. Also, there are Gestaltists who have used techniques inappropriate to their basic theory.

Identifying Features

A process-oriented holistic approach (includes mind, body, culture); multi-systemic; phenomenological; humanistic; based consistently in the here-and-now client experience; experiment-focused; a longer-term methodology; action-based.

Reflections

It's important for students to appreciate the use of techniques in Gestalt Therapy but take serious note that simply learning them isn't what the approach is about; they are employed in the context of a strong therapeutic relationship and counselling process. The single purpose of learning a technique is to help the client develop self-awareness and understanding, not because you consider it's a good thing to do or you can't think of anything else. This can happen with mediocre practitioners who push ideas on to clients instead of allowing them to decide for themselves.

To be a good Gestalt practitioner you require particularly high-quality observation skills, in my view, since you need to be able to spot any small, even tiny, physical sign in your client. This enables you to ask about it, then explore and discuss underlying feelings, emotions and thoughts before considering possible changes for enhanced functioning.

I respect the clear guidance given to Gestalt practitioners, i.e., who they should work with and when. This calls for significant self-awareness, self-honesty and self-discipline in students and qualified practitioners (in all approaches, actually!).

I find Gestalt to be an interesting and challenging therapeutic approach.

▬▬▬ Summary ▬▬▬▬▬▬▬▬▬▬▬

Gestalt is a distinctive, experiential longer-term therapy where both the focus and methodology is based on developing client self-awareness as the core component for progress and resolution of underlying issues. It demands high degrees of practitioner self-awareness, honesty and observation skills. Practitioners only work with clients who are appropriate for their competence and experience levels. Given these caveats, this process-approach can be applied across a wide range of clients, issues and age groups, to some depth.

Learning Ideas

1   Sit or lie comfortably in a quiet, dimly lit room with your arms loosely by your sides. Close your eyes and breathe deeply and slowly for a few minutes. Focus on your physical state, trying to notice any tension spots in your body. If you find any, continue to breathe as just suggested and ponder what underlying psychological reasons are causing the bodily tautness. This is an exercise in becoming more physically self-aware in order to understand yourself better.

2   What are your introjections and blocks to greater awareness?

3   Revision

   a   Make sure you are well grounded in Gestalt Theory.

   b   Study and understand the principles of: Dialogical Psychotherapy; Gestalt Practice; Gestalt Awareness Practice.

   c   Check your knowledge and understanding of these terms: holistic; phenomenology; existentialism; experiential; humanistic.

 ## Suggested Reading

Brownell, P. (2010) *Gestalt Therapy: A Guide to Contemporary Practice.* New York: Springer.

Clarkson, P. (2004) *Gestalt Counselling in Action.* London: Sage.

Mann, D. (2010) *Gestalt Therapy: 100 Key Points and Techniques.* Hove: Routledge.

9

Integrative Counselling

Integrative counselling wasn't 'invented' as such; it came about via ideas merging from different theorists over roughly the last 60–70 years. For example, the philosophy of Carl Rogers is significant (say, 1940s onwards) since he espoused the therapeutic benefits of treating clients as discrete individuals and working in a person-centred fashion. Gerard Egan was influenced by Rogers, introducing the Developmental Approach to counselling (1970s), which drew on both the person-centred and cognitive behavioural orientations. During the 1970s the *cognitive revolution* took place, another influence on the concept of incorporating and merging ideas, methods and techniques from different therapeutic perspectives. In the 1990s in the UK, Sue Culley worked on her integrative model which aims to teach a range of counselling skills to students wishing to become counselling practitioners, without necessarily basing them in any core theoretical viewpoint.

The therapeutic world has witnessed a developing movement towards more integrated approaches since the early 1980s. It's grounded in the idea of combining parts of different orientations in order to produce more complete theoretical models and effective treatments and procedures. A major reason for this trend is the acknowledgement that no single approach, model or theory is encompassing enough to cover for the complexities of human beings and the issues they have.

There are now established therapeutically integrated approaches such as Transactional Analysis (TA), Rational Emotive Behaviour Therapy (REBT), Cognitive Analytical Therapy (CAT), Cognitive Behaviour Therapy (CBT) and the Developmental Approach (although Egan referred to his methodology as *systematic eclecticism*). I believe they could be described as *structured integrative therapies*.

In a more general sense Integrative counselling generally refers to a merging of two or more therapies or the integration of ideas or techniques from a range of approaches, which can be called *technical eclecticism*. Therefore, the term *Integrative counselling* can be used to describe any multi-modal approach that combines therapies or takes ideas from them.

At this point we need to remember that the integrative perspective considers that no one theoretical standpoint works for every client. The aim is to 'customise' the therapy to meet the needs of each client, which is consistent with the humanistic/Existential counselling philosophies. However, a fundamental cognitive format to the therapeutic process is vital and is usually made up of three or more stages, but it must be flexible enough to be adapted to each individual client at any stage in the counselling work. For example, Culley's model contains the following stages and practitioner competencies for each one:

1   Beginning Stage (it's about establishing the relationship, understanding and defining issues, producing a client assessment and agreeing a contract): attending and active listening skills; restating,

87

paraphrasing, summarising; probing questions and statements; concrete examples; non-verbal communication.

2 Middle Stage (it's about reassessing issues, establishing and maintaining a working therapeutic relationship, plus implementing the contract): same skills as in first stage.

3 Ending Stage (it's about deciding on constructive changes, transferring learning of relevant material from the process to the client, both parties evaluating the work and concluding the contract): same skills as in first and second stages.

It's important at this juncture to reflect on the words *integrative* and *eclectic* to avoid confusion, since they are not interchangeable as some students and practitioners mistakenly believe. Palmer and Woolfe (1999) say: 'Integration suggests that the elements are part of one combined approach to theory and practice, as opposed to eclecticism, which draws *ad hoc* from several approaches in the approach to a particular case.'

Integrative practitioners are often theoretically based in one or more viewpoints, blending these theories together in their work, also wanting to know *how* and *why* a technique or method works.

Eclectic practitioners are primarily focused on what works and tend to mix aspects and techniques of whatever theoretical standpoints fit the work with a client. They are interested in *what* and *how* something succeeds without necessarily having a formal theoretical foundation.

There are ways to develop Integrative counselling practice and four major ones are:

1 Common Factors: involves checking through different theoretical approaches seeking common elements which are considered at least as effective as the specific factors that separate one methodology from another.

2 Theoretical Integration: refers to a theoretical creation beyond the mere blending of techniques and aims to combine the best components of two or more theoretical approaches, believing this will

result in better outcomes, and not those obtained from relying on single-base theories alone.

3   Assimilative Integration: relates to being based in one approach and incorporating ideas, methods, techniques from other perspectives.

4   Technical Eclecticism (which Egan described as *random eclecticism*): tends to focus more on selecting a variety of methods and techniques from a range of theoretical orientations without having a formal therapeutic base.

Integrative counselling doesn't aim to change a person; instead it attempts to re-integrate their best features for better functioning.

Some Big Names

Beutler, L.E. (1980s onwards): American psychologist; he developed Systematic Treatment Selection (STS).

Brooks-Harris, J.E. (1980s onwards): American psychologist; he produced Multitheoretical Psychotherapy (MPT).

Nelson-Jones, R. (1980s onwards): British counselling psychologist; he developed the Lifeskills Helping Model.

Prochaska, J.O. (born 1943): American psychologist; he introduced the Transtheoretical Model of Behaviour Change (TTM) in 1977.

Some Big Ideas

Blending approaches to meet individual differences/needs; the practitioner–client relationship; eclecticism; syncretism; structured integrative counselling.

How it Works

A thoughtful and competent Integrative practitioner works with client cognitions, emotions, feelings, actions and behaviours in the therapeutic process because these are considered prime components of the human psyche.

In the following example I utilise technical eclecticism methodology and Culley's model. In the opening stage the practitioner uses core concepts such as empathy, respect and genuineness to establish a sound therapeutic relationship, and exploration skills to open up the client in order for both parties to clearly understand the issues which have brought the client into counselling. Once this is done the practitioner makes an assessment and both parties agree on a contract. Further work is conducted to strengthen the dynamic and broaden client perspective by reassessing their issues. Then the contract is ready for implementation. This involves making specific decisions on desired changes, putting them into action and evaluating progress as the client moves towards goals and conclusion of the therapeutic process. Throughout this scenario the practitioner can appropriately provide psycho-educational interventions so the client's knowledge-base and self-understanding grows.

 A brief example

A new client suffers from anxiety, which affects all areas of their life (late 20s, single, employed full-time, sharing a flat with a friend): 'I'm a bit of a worrier.' They want to feel more at ease with themselves and not get so 'stressed about everything'.

In the first session you invite the client to tell the story of what brings them to counselling. At this time your aim is to help them feel secure and accepted, not threatened or judged. Essentially, you utilise a *Person-Centred* approach to establish a conducive potential therapeutic environment. Sessions progress at the client's pace and they gradually open up to you, beginning to explore themselves, their feelings, emotions, thoughts and behaviours. You might incorporate *Psychodynamic/CAT* ideas such as attachment/early relationships, defence mechanisms, transference and the unconscious, while also drawing on *TA's* Parent–Adult–Child and life-script concepts so they start to learn about the origins of their anxieties, 'worries' and 'doubts'. For your assessment and contract, you decide to use a functional analysis and clinical formulation method taken from *Behaviour Therapy*.

As the process continues perhaps you notice the client is giving you cognitive responses when you ask feelings-based questions as you explore the caring but sometimes stressful advice-giving and instruction of their parent, and how the client feels about it as they get older. You address this with them and they say 'I don't feel anything'. Perhaps you gently challenge the client and introduce some *Gestalt* techniques to assist them to become aware of underlying emotions, which leads to greater client self-understanding.

Over time the client becomes more comfortable with the counselling and you both consider their thinking patterns and options for change. This could involve you employing concepts and methods from such as *Cognitive Therapy*, like automatic thoughts, or *CBT*, e.g., cognitive distortions and the ABC format, and/or irrational beliefs and the ABCDE construct from *REBT*. Perhaps you help them broaden their perspective on how they live in a way that allows negative thoughts and actions to dominate them, which relates to their anxiety, lack of confidence in decision-making and assertiveness, and underlying feelings of dissatisfaction and frustration. You employ concepts like self-states and reciprocal roles from *CAT*. With greater self-understanding about unhelpful thinking, actions and relationship dynamics, allied to a strong therapeutic relationship, the client feels ready to attempt practical changes. Let's say you both confer about this next stage and opt for some straightforward behavioural changes from *Behaviour Therapy*.

(Continued)

(Continued)

You put these into operation, with the client performing active homework tasks, like not always automatically answering the phone when friends call, even if it is at a convenient time; this could be seen as a behavioural experiment from *Behaviour Therapy*. The client reports there are no negative repercussions from friends, evidencing that they don't need to impose 'musts', 'oughts' and 'shoulds' about being eternally available to others; this relates to *Gestalt Counselling*.

From this, you work on other change topics until the client is ready to face their life in a more authentic fashion. At this point you utilise the method of Goodbye letters from *CAT*, offering this option to the client, who agrees, so bringing the counselling process to a satisfactory conclusion. You offer a couple of follow-up sessions but the client declines, stating they feel 'more grown up' and self-sufficient than when they started, and are confident about their abilities to cope in the future.

Who it's For

This is an interesting matter because Integrative practitioners seem to focus on the potential for a strong therapeutic relationship with individual clients as the key factor for effective counselling, rather than claiming efficacy with particular groups or in particular settings, e.g., children, mental health clients, education, the workplace. Instead, in the initial session with a client, the practitioner seeks positive or negative factors that will indicate the viability of working together. If the indications are negative, the ethical practitioner refers the client on at the earliest possibility, which, of course, constitutes good practice.

The approach is appropriate for use across diverse backgrounds and ancestries, and should work with people of different ages.

As with many therapies, it might be unsuitable for those with certain brain conditions, substance misuse issues or low motivation to participate in change processes.

Critical Considerations

Integrative students and practitioners who don't fully understand the philosophy and practice of the approach may think they are operating appropriately whereas they are simply 'grabbing' techniques they like (*syncretism*), or are uncertain about what to do at a certain point in the therapy. Effectively, they are just muddling through the counselling process. Critics argue that this may be due to a lack of a substantial theoretical base from one or more approaches. Moreover, undisciplined *eclectic* practice can be an excuse for not developing a proper rationale for using certain concepts and methods related to them. Indeed, it could be argued that without a sound theoretical foundation and rationale a practitioner can end up simply employing random techniques with all clients, reflecting their own biases and preferences.

Another way of looking at this is to conclude that the blending of theoretical constructs from two or more modalities and developing a sound working rationale presents more of a challenge than just utilising techniques from different approaches as and when you decide to.

With reference to supportive evidence for Integrative counselling approaches, more research needs to be done regarding the effectiveness of such models. It would appear more straightforward to contemplate investigating evidence for the usefulness of carefully constructed approaches than the looser eclectic practices.

Identifying Features

Humanistic; no required theoretical base (though many training courses do include a theoretical core); practitioners develop their own counselling style; some practitioners describe themselves as eclectic; short-term and longer-term work; skills-based.

Reflections

In my view as practitioner, lecturer, tutor, clinical supervisor and assessor, having a clear primary theoretical base gives students a sound foundation for their work.

Also, take time to consider the amount of knowledge required to be a quality Integrative counsellor, particularly if you decide to follow an approach employing technical eclecticism. If we only consider the example above, such practitioners, I maintain, would need to know and understand in depth, the Person-Centred Approach, Gestalt Therapy, Cognitive Therapy, Behaviour Therapy, Psychodynamic Counselling, Transactional Analysis, Cognitive Behaviour Therapy, Rational Emotive Behaviour Therapy, in addition to Integrative philosophy and principles.... That's a lot to digest, comprehend and integrate as you set out to practise and develop your own counselling style.

Summary

Integrative counselling operates from a humanistic philosophy, believing no single theoretical orientation is effective for all clients since we are all individuals, and so counsellors should be able to 'customise' their practice to meet the complexities of each client they work with. There are a number of ways for students and practitioners to develop their own therapeutic styles. Some are more obviously integrative, while others are more accurately described as eclectic. The approach is employed in both short-term and longer-term contexts, and is skills-based.

In the UK, Integrative counselling started to take off from around the 1990s.

In my experience, in a number of relevant professional roles, the quality of Integrative counselling training courses is variable.

Learning Ideas

1   Check the four ways of developing Integrative counselling practice. Think about which alternative(s) you might prefer or feel drawn to, and why. After this, write down which format(s) you've chosen and be clear with yourself about your preference(s).

2   Reflect on different theoretical orientations and which one(s) you are attracted to, plus those you have less interest in. Think about why you have made these choices – what might they indicate about you as a person?

3   Revision

   a   Make sure you are clear about the meanings of the following: theoretical integration; assimilative integration; technical eclecticism; common factors.

   b   Check out and understand the following approaches: Systematic Treatment Selection (STS); the Transtheoretical Model of Behaviour Change (TMM); Multitheoretical Psychotherapy (MPT).

   c   Consider and explain the general differences between *integrative* and *eclectic*.

 **Suggested Reading**

Corey, G. (2008) *The Art of Integrative Counselling*. Pacific Grove, CA: Brooks-Cole.

Culley, S. (2011) *Integrative Counselling*. London: Sage.

Nelson-Jones, R. (2006) *Human Relationships Skills*. Hove: Routledge.

10

Person-Centred Counselling

Origins and Background

Carl Rogers (1923–1987) was an American psychologist, psychotherapist, educator and psychotherapeutic researcher who also formulated a theory of personality development. He made the bold and critical statement that psychoanalytical and behavioural schools of thought and therapy were diagnostic and directive, with practitioners presenting as powerful 'experts', which inhibited clients from personal growth and fulfilling their psychological potential. He was ostracised for a substantial amount of his career by a number of his orthodox peers.

Through his own practice experience, Rogers concluded that, generally, clients were capable of finding solutions for themselves but might benefit from a supportive facilitating practitioner, a *helper* rather than a directing authority figure. He maintained that given the right life conditions, people will thrive and grow in an interpersonally and socially harmonious manner. He posited that this behaviour is directly related to his key idea known as the *actualising tendency*, which states that a human organism's innate inclination is to organise and lead life in an enhancing way. Further, the Person-Centred Approach (PCA) says there is a psychological dimension of this concept, the *self-actualising tendency*, which is affected by our life experiences and other people.

Rogers believed the quality of the *therapeutic relationship*, progress and outcomes is strongly influential for clients dealing with their issues. Therefore, the role of the practitioner is critical in the counselling process. He said they should focus more on their state of *being* with clients, not on *doing*. By creating a facilitative environment, supported clients become empowered within an equal relationship to explore, recognise, face their issues and then move towards a *fully functioning* existence. Practitioners put the philosophy into practice by behaving in a certain way instead of employing a panoply of techniques within a given number of structured sessions.

A fundamental of Rogerian and person-centred philosophy and practice is the belief that it's the interpersonal relationship between practitioner and client which leads to growth, resolution and attaining a person's psychological health.

Rogers said there are certain *core conditions* required in this helping approach:

- Empathy: the practitioner's cognitive and emotional understanding of the client; seeing from the client's point of view/frame of reference.
- Unconditional Positive Regard (UPR): includes concepts like respect, acceptance and non-judgementalism emanating from practitioner to client.
- Congruence: a sense of practitioner genuineness, honesty and consistency of manner experienced by the client.

Three other concepts are now also considered important as additional necessary and sufficient conditions for client personal growth:

1 Therapist–client psychological contact: this is about how each party perceives the other, and needs to be constructive enough to give the process a chance.

2   Client incongruence or vulnerability: this can cause anxiety, which hopefully motivates the client to stay in the therapeutic relationship.
3   Client perception: of the practitioner's empathy, congruence and UPR.

In addition, Rogers believed clients need to be convinced of a practitioner's total trustworthiness.

Rogers first introduced a *non-directive* therapeutic approach (1930s–1940s) before presenting Client-Centred therapy (1950s–1960s), then expanding the concept into Person-Centred Counselling. He believed the philosophy and principles were relevant to other spheres, e.g., child-rearing/family work, education, the workplace, social work, group-work, conflict situations. Consequently, the Person-Centred Approach (PCA) evolved.

Rogers' beliefs were judged by many to constitute revolutionary thinking, some describing him as the founder of humanistic counselling. Later in his career he included a spiritual dimension to his theoretical perspective.

Two fundamental ideas to understand are:

1   Self-concept: the view that we construct of ourselves. It directly relates to our inherent need for approval/positive regard and human relationships, which commences in early childhood. It develops from experiences with other people and how the growing individual evaluates them.

The impact of *conditional* and *unconditional positive regard* is fundamental to this development. Conditional positive regard comes from the values, expectations and demands of significant others, which we internalise (introjections); then we tend to like ourselves dependent on how people behave towards us. This is called having *external locus/loci of evaluation*, from which grows an *ideal self* (one we try to be to gain approval from others, a sort of perfect self). But living according to the wishes of others can cause us internal pressures, and particularly powerful ones can lead to psychological conflicts and splits; this is at the expense of our *real/organismic self*. Psychological disturbance can occur from this, being consolidated if we continue to be dependent on the opinions and judgements of others.

Unconditional positive regard pertains to our self-concept being nurtured from an early age and growing with a sense of freedom without undue pressures put on us to conform to the demands of other people. Such an environment encourages the growth of the organismic self, self-acceptance, higher levels of self-esteem and an *internal locus of evaluation*.

2 Conditions of worth: values, expectations, assumptions, demands of significant others we put on ourselves (real or imagined).

PCA recognises two defence mechanisms we may employ to protect ourselves against internalised stressors which can cause psychological dysfunction, and even breakdown:

1 Denial: avoiding recognition of any conscious experience that threatens the ideal self.
2 Distortion: when a threatening experience comes into awareness but only in a way that maintains a person's approval-seeking ideal self.

Some Big Names

Devonshire, C. (1960s onwards): British psychologist; colleague of Rogers; he founded the Facilitator Development Institute (FDI) in 1974, introducing PCA ideas to the UK.
Dewey, J. (1859–1952): leading American philosopher (1920s onwards), psychologist, educationalist; he helped develop Functional psychology and the theory of *pragmatism*; interested

in broadening ideas relating to democracy (especially in education).

Porter, E.H. (1914–1987): American psychologist; peer of Rogers, he researched Client-Centred work, finding evidence for its efficacy.

Rank, O. (1884–1939): German psychoanalyst, psychotherapist, educator; he was instrumental in Rogers formulating his own ideas and approach.

Some Big Ideas

Client-led; humanistic/existential/phenomenological; distortion and denial (includes repression); introjections; reflection; practitioner being not doing.

How it Works

PCA is about communicating the attitudes which are necessary and sufficient to help clients move towards full functioning and psychological health.

It's crucial that a PCA practitioner prepares and operates with the correct mindset, i.e., as a helper and facilitator for the client, not as an expert or authority figure who has all the answers. We should also remember that Rogers didn't want practitioners to copy him; instead he encouraged students and relevant others to work with the philosophy, values and principles of a person-centred approach within their own practice style. He stressed that for practitioners PCA encompasses a way of *being* not *doing* (as in a set methodology utilising a particular range of techniques and exercises).

The PCA paradigm can be encapsulated by certain steps taken in the therapeutic process:

1   An individual decides to attend for counselling.
2   The practitioner explains PCA and their role in the process.
3   The practitioner shows the core conditions from the outset in order to establish and maintain a conducive environment for the client to explore and express themselves as they seek to resolve issues.
4   The practitioner intervenes appropriately, helping the client to recognise and face negative feelings, thoughts, behaviours.
5   After reaching a point of understanding and clarity about their negative issues, the client starts to feel more positive about themselves and the possibilities for full psychological functioning.
6   The practitioner accepts and relates to the client's healthier thoughts and emotions in the same fashion they do to negative ones.
7   Client insight, understanding and self-acceptance grow along with possible courses of action for constructive change.
8   The client takes action towards full functioning, which involves reviews of progress and moves towards a declining need for help.

 A brief example

A new client suffers from anxiety, which affects all areas of their life (late 20s, single, employed full-time, shares a flat with a friend): 'I'm a bit of a worrier.' They want to feel more at ease with themselves and 'not get so stressed about everything'.

Let's suppose you start by explaining to the client how PCA practitioners help but don't advise, guide, direct or instruct. You seek clarification about what brings the client to you and what they hope for from the process.

In the early sessions you work hard to show trustworthiness as you establish the core conditions for a strong therapeutic relationship.

You employ basic counselling skills, including reflecting of client emotions, paraphrasing what you've heard and seeking clarification of anything you haven't quite understood. This shows you pay attention; it also indicates respect for, and valuing of, the client. In such an accepting and non-judgemental environment the client slowly relaxes. They have some initial discomfort from exploring themselves to find understanding and answers, instead of a powerful, decisive parent-figure providing the solutions. However, you are consistent in your role and via your empathy and unconditional positive regard the client explores further, coming to a point where they realise they have a fear of being unlovable and are scared of rejection. They gradually understand they go along with what people want and say in order to be liked, i.e., they feel valued if they conform to the wishes and opinions of significant others. This relates to the origin of their anxiety.

You continue to evidence the core conditions, earning the trust of the client, who becomes more comfortable with self-exploration.

Let's say you notice and feed back to them that they have stopped asking what you think and their irritability with your lack of guidance or answers has decreased. The client hadn't realised this change and they reflect on it, concluding that they don't feel criticised, which is how they might have interpreted such comments previously. Your manner helps their self-acceptance grow and they muse over underlying emotional guilt about sometimes feeling annoyed when their parent or a significant person gives advice or direction. They come to realise their parent loves them and wants to protect them from life's dangers, but the annoyance relates to part of the client wanting to make their own decisions without feeling guilty about upsetting the parent. We might say their *real self* is emerging.

During the next phase of the process, encouraged by your empowering, supportive practice style, the client asserts new ways of thinking and evidence of self-acceptance appears, e.g., 'Well, I'm entitled to an opinion like my friends are – they don't apologise for saying how they feel, so maybe I don't have to, either...'.

(Continued)

103

(Continued)

From here the client feels confident enough to contemplate changes to the way they interact with important people in their life, e.g., 'If my boss is off-hand with me again, I'll try not to take it so personally. After all, I know I'm conscientious and good at my job, so maybe the way they behave is more about them than me...'.

As changes are introduced, you help the client monitor and evaluate their inner responses to the new behaviours by reflecting what they say to you, and exploring any quandaries, dilemmas, uncertainties they have.

Within the safe and accepting environment expressed by you consistently displaying the core conditions, the client frees their real self, progressing towards *self-actualisation* and psychologically healthier living.

Who it's For

Hypothetically, PCA can benefit all ages and across cultures so long as the core conditions are continually evident to clients.

Critics argue that the approach might not work with certain serious mental health conditions (e.g., schizoid personalities). However, PCA practitioners operate in this sphere, sometimes establishing relationship with 'hard-to-reach' patients/clients (sort of 'breaking the ice', if you will) who may then transfer to another modality such as CBT, CAT or Psychodynamics.

For clients who seek immediate solutions to their issues, they might prefer a focused short-term methodology.

Identifying Features

Practitioner qualities and core conditions more important than a formal methodology and technique-based approach;

usually longer-term; transferable to other settings; taught and utilised around the world.

Critical Considerations

Significant research studies have been conducted supporting the constructive effects of PCA core conditions and use of particular communication skills at appropriate points of the counselling process.

Some critics view PCA as passive, but supporters point out experiential-based studies revealing client acknowledgement of its potency and action.

Others have incorrectly contended that Rogers failed to acknowledge the unconscious, since he directly recognised the concept in later writings.

It's been suggested that an 'over-use' of *reflection* can irritate and frustrate clients. However, inappropriate utilisation of techniques by practitioners from any orientation is certainly not unknown...

Another criticism is that PCA's core conditions allow for a lot of interpretation which might cause difficulty in measuring effectiveness. Further, some argue it's impossible to *always* use the three core conditions equally at the same time...

In response to theologians claiming PCA doesn't account for the concept of *evil* and baser parts of human behaviour, Rogers said we can have a self-actualising tendency plus forces from the world that bring negativity into our lives, psyches and behaviours.

Reflections

If we consider PCA deeply, it's clear how challenging it is for any (potential) practitioner – consistently evidencing the core conditions as the means not only to establish a strong therapeutic relationship with clients but to assist them in exploring, recognising, addressing, changing themselves to enable their actualising tendency to flourish so they can become more fully functioning in life and relationships. The approach is much more demanding than simply learning a structured process and set of techniques to employ with clients because it implements Rogers' theory of human relationships, which includes our inherent inclination to have harmonious, accepting dynamics with other people. When clients arrive for counselling they are in a state of psychological disturbance and the PCA practitioner has to show them complete acceptance, regard, respect and empathy for the client's view of themselves and the world in order to provide a safe and engaging environment for the client to begin their work. Integral here is the necessity to be non-judgemental about every client!

Summary

PCA is a stand-out therapy, in that practitioners operate via actually implementing the philosophical values as the means to help clients address and resolve issues, and so progress to full psychological health and life functioning. It's a demanding discipline for any (prospective) practitioner, requiring great self-control to keep their own views, attitudes, judgements, biases out of the counselling process, and not to be guides, instructors, advisers or directors of their clients. PCA values and principles have been successfully transferred to a variety of contexts outside the counselling sphere as well as being incorporated into other therapeutic modalities.

Learning Ideas

1 Ponder the following proposition: we can't truly accept other people unless we truly accept ourselves. Explore your reactions to this suggestion and write down your thoughts on the matter.

2 Explore the levels of core conditions within you regarding this hypothetical client: an individual presents for counselling with the following issue: they have been convicted of child sexual abuse (touching a 5 year old) and have agreed to be referred.

    Look at yourself honestly; could you work with this client? If yes, explain to yourself why. If no, why not? Would you leave it there or explore your reactions further with someone else? If so, who? If not, why not?

3 Revision

    a Make sure you know and understand the relationship between the self-concept and conditions of worth, and how they affect personal development.

    b Be clear about why *practitioner self-acceptance* is key to quality counselling.

    c Consider whether the PCA recognition of two defence mechanisms is broad enough in your view.

 ### Suggested Reading

Casemore, R. (2006) *Person-Centred Counselling in a Nutshell.* London: Sage.

Mearns, D. and Thorne, B. (2007) *Person-Centred Counselling in Action* (3rd edition). London: Sage.

Wilkins, P. (2010) *Person-Centred Therapy: 100 Key Points.* Hove: Routledge.

11

Psychodynamic Counselling and Psychotherapy

Origins and Background

Psychodynamic counselling and psychotherapy is the child of psychoanalysis, whose original introduction is credited to Sigmund Freud around the turn of the 20th century. During this period a profusion of psychoanalytic theorists and practitioners appeared. Today, psychoanalysis maintains itself as a discipline in its own right while providing the foundation ideas of its broader and more flexible derivative, the psychodynamic approach.

Psychodynamic counselling gives major significance to *relationships*, and within this, *early relationships* and experiences of a person which shape psychological development, maturation and later adult dynamics. Thus, individuals are influenced by underlying emotions, thoughts and images. A person's development and future functioning will be determined by these experiences. If they were negative, then adult relationships and the internal *self* can be impaired, even if the experiences are not remembered, or apparently felt in adverse ways. This relates to psychic functioning and the concepts of the *conscious* and *unconscious* (also called the *subconscious*) mind.

The aim of psychodynamics is to make the unconscious, conscious, so we can understand then reduce or rid ourselves of negative early experiences and thus operate better. The theory is that if we allow ourselves to become aware of unhelpful behavioural patterns and face the accompanying issues, we can take healthier control of ourselves, including the ability to have sound adult relationships.

An influential concept here is *Object Relations Theory* (some call it *id psychology*), which refers to how an infant mind develops in its world and starts to form its personal identity. Some of the major contributors to the evolution of the theory and practice include Melanie Klein (1882–1960), Donald Winnicott (1896–1971) and Ronald Fairbairn (1889–1964).

'Objects' can be defined as people or things a child relates to (animate or inanimate, real or imagined). Object relations begin from our early dynamics and activities with significant adults (usually care-givers, primarily a mother figure). While resultant behaviours can change via our life experiences, nevertheless these early relationships often remain influential, even powerful, in adulthood. A related idea is that of *unconscious phantasy*, which pertains to imagined happenings, consequences, outcomes and how we internally see people and things in our minds. This is a key element in developing our thinking capabilities.

There are a number of other relevant ideas associated with Object Relations, including:

- Part objects: very young children initially relate to parts of a person, e.g., the mouth which feeds or scares, a hand which strokes or hits.
- Whole objects: another person bestowed with emotions, capabilities, vulnerabilities, rights, etc.
- External objects: people, places, things the growing infant relates to.
- Internal objects: these are an individual's inner representations which reflect the way they relate to other people or things, and can be ideas, imaginings, memories which impact upon their

psychological harmony and development (bear in mind these objects can be perceived as good or bad).

- Transitional objects: first or early external possessions, e.g., a blanket, which can be stress-reducing for the child because it lessens separation anxiety in relation to a primary care-giver.
- The Self: simply put, the conscious/unconscious internal view of oneself.
- Individuation: roughly, it means gradual maturational separation from the care-giver as the child becomes an individual in their own right.

Attachment Theory (introduced by John Bowlby) widened and deepened our comprehension of Object Relations, both playing significant roles in the development and practice of modern psychodynamic counselling and therapy.

Object Relations and Attachment Theory are considered major theoretical bases of modern psychodynamics, alongside the three psychoanalytical schools of thought which underpin the general approach, i.e., Freudian, Jungian and Kleinian, with their traditionally significant concepts. These include: *transference*, which is when a client transfers emotions for a third person on to the practitioner; *counter-transference*, which is a similar process but from practitioner to client; *resistance*, which is a general term referring to when clients avoid facing subjects which obstruct constructive personal growth and relates to a range of *defence mechanisms* used by people unwilling to address troubling issues.

(Please note here that many psychodynamic training courses and practitioners maintain differences between the two terms: *counselling* is viewed as applicable to lower-level issues requiring less time spent on them and sessions are usually once a week; *psychotherapy* is for deep-rooted, more challenging issues and can last for years, perhaps taking up to five sessions per week.)

Some Big Names

Bion, W.R. (1897–1979): British psychoanalyst; he did early work on group processes and group dynamics; influenced the development of group psychotherapy and encounter groups.

Bowlby, J.M. (1907–1990): British psychologist, psychiatrist and psychoanalyst; an early researcher into Attachment Theory and child development; some of his ideas on child–mother relationships led to him being marginalised by mainstream psychoanalysis.

Freud, A. (1895–1982): Austrian psychoanalyst; daughter of Sigmund Freud; one of the founders of psychoanalytical Child Psychology; did significant work on expanding the range of defence mechanisms; helped develop Ego Psychology.

Von Brucke, E.W.R. (1819–1892): German physician and physiologist; an influence on his student, Sigmund Freud, which ultimately led to the development of psychodynamics.

Some Big Ideas

Self-regulation; archetypes; insight; psychopathology; dream analysis; free association; containment; interpretation; dissonance; catharsis; endings.

How it Works

The aim is to establish a safe and consistent therapeutic environment so practitioner and client can explore the origins of client issues. This is accomplished by examining early relationships and working out how they play out in adulthood. *Unconscious* aspects of the *psyche* are brought to the surface for greater self-understanding by the client, who is then better placed to manage themselves well in the future, gradually reducing the need for practitioner input.

 A brief example

(You utilise your own therapeutic style which includes aspects of the three main schools of psychodynamic thought. Imagine you work with this client for, say, 60 weekly sessions.)

A new client suffers from anxiety, which affects all areas of their life (late 20s, single, employed full-time, shares a flat with a friend): 'I'm a bit of a worrier.' They want to feel more at ease with themselves and 'not get so stressed about everything'.

Before commencement your mindset needs to be in place; you must be prepared to utilise your own reactions to the client and constructively use such as defence mechanisms and transference behaviours they bring into sessions. You start by explaining how you work, clarifying your rules around session times and fees (if they're paying). You conduct an assessment, including what the client wants from counselling.

Let's imagine the process follows these lines: by employing core conditions and basic counselling skills you assist the client to settle into the initial sessions, inviting them to tell you about their background, history and childhood. Simultaneously, you educate the client about such as Object Relations, Attachment Theory, resistance and defence mechanisms to help understanding of their inner self, and how types of relationship patterns and associated issues emerge and impact how people live.

The client tells you they have a loving, protective parent who brought them up (Parent 1), and who '…always looks out for me…' and '…only wants the best for me…'. There is a second parent (Parent 2), who has been absent from the client's life from a very early age, and appears intermittently, but is '…selfish, and doesn't really care about me…'.

112

The client explores and reflects on early experiences and feelings towards their parents, showing anger and resentment for Parent 2, plus feelings of rejection and abandonment, while being totally positive about Parent 1. As you proceed you get resistance and anger from the client as they avoid anything that could be interpreted as critical of Parent 1, e.g., when you offer 'over protective' for consideration. Also, you mention the client possibly having rejection and abandonment issues, relating this to their low levels of self-esteem and ego strength. Defensively, the client *transfers* their anger with Parent 2 on to you. You share how it feels for you to receive these emotional waves from the client, assuring them you won't reject or abandon them, relating their emotions and behaviours to unconscious feelings about Parent 2.

Over time the client trusts you more, tentatively approaching the impact of their early relationship with Parent 1. *Rationalisation, denial, procrastination* appear as the client defends the parent. Gradually, you begin to feel guilty about asking and challenging the client about Parent 1, and you don't know why. You share your feelings with the client and further discussion ensues. Then the client discloses they have guilt feelings if they consider saying 'bad things' about their loving parent (some *projective identification* has occurred). However, your shared feelings assist the client's unconscious emotions to become conscious. They are now more self-aware and progress continues.

Your sharing helps the client relax with increased trust as they venture into the taboo area. At this point you remind them of the concept of *individuation* and personal progress to independent living and a freer self.

Sessions proceed. The client delves into self re-evaluation with enhanced understanding of underlying issues with both parents that are now conscious and acknowledged. The client appreciates how their development, attitudes, behaviours and self-image were affected by early relationships. Their anxieties, lack of confidence, need to be popular and liked, compliance and conformity, and tendency to overt emotional over-reaction have all surfaced and are worked through. They feel able to separate from Parent 1 without feeling guilty about betraying or abandoning this original, loving primary carer.

(Continued)

(Continued)

The client reaches a stage where their self-image is positive and their ego has been strengthened to an extent where counselling can conclude.

Who it's For

Psychodynamic practitioners have maintained a strong presence in the UK health system, often working alongside clinical psychologists and psychiatrists (though CBT approaches have threatened that domination over the last five years or so, due to a perceived effectiveness within short-term provision, so making it relatively more cost-effective). Practitioners work with children, adolescents and adults with mild to severe psychological health conditions. The approach is also prevalent in wider associated helping arenas, e.g., schools, colleges, universities, Social Services, social care settings, family work, community counselling agencies.

Psychodynamics may not be the most appropriate choice for people who want an immediate solution to difficulties they're encountering or for those disinclined to explore their inner selves to understand the deeper aspects and roots of their issues. Also, individuals with substance misuse issues may prefer other more obviously structured and 'concrete' methodologies.

Clients who are likely to benefit from this approach include people who: want to reflect on themselves and understand how they relate to others; know and wish to face deep-rooted issues; have experienced significant negative changes in their lives which are difficult to deal with; seek meaning and purpose in their existence.

Identifying Features

Evolved from psychoanalysis; emphasis on the past and how childhood experiences impact on development and adult relationships; usually longer-term, though there is a short-term version; stresses the importance of the unconscious and bringing it into consciousness; practitioners develop their own therapeutic style; practitioner sharing of their own self as part of the counselling process.

Critical Considerations

Some critics say there is a lack of Object Relations long-term studies into early development and how it might be affected in larger family groups where there are numerous parental figures. On the other hand, studies into Attachment Theory seem to support the validity of developmental processes put forward by Object Relations.

Another Object Relations criticism is that it doesn't cater for social norms and structures.

It's accurate to say that much criticism actually derives from within psychoanalysis/psychodynamics rather than external sources; the overall approach has different dimensions and schools of thought, numerous and diverse emphases and nuances, all of which have their own eager supporters and enthusiastic adversaries.

Reflections

Without deeply delving into this particular point (sadly, there isn't scope in this book), the concept of practitioners expressing their personal reactions to client comments and behaviours is an interesting one which goes beyond the idea of *practitioner self-disclosure* utilised in some other approaches. In my view, if a practitioner gives their personal view about something during counselling it can certainly have a powerful impact – positively *or* negatively.... Therefore, *how*, *when* and *why* we say things is important, otherwise the most well-intentioned of words can be counter-productive at the very least. Caution and self-awareness are vital here. Such interventions must be for the benefit of the process and desired outcomes.

Similarly, *interpretation* can be a useful tool of practitioners but there are risks if the interpretations are based on personal biases, prejudices, values or assumptions – so, be very careful about employing them until you know and understand yourself well!

There are two practice areas that can be challenging for psychodynamic students and professionals:

1   Session times and time-keeping: basically, the contention is that establishing firm appointment days and times are helpful in creating safety and security in clients, and combat such as client avoidance, the need for control, or to be powerful. Thus, some training courses teach students not to allow the rearrangement of session times, other than, say, for practitioner unavailability. That's something for you to ponder...

Also, if a client comes early, the session starts on time; if they're late, the session, similarly, finishes at the allotted time.

2   Fee payments: again, some courses are unequivocal about this matter, i.e., the client must pay for any missed sessions, even emergencies, a family death, hospitalisation, etc., though they may miss weeks or months of sessions – think about how you explain that to a prospective client...

Psychodynamic (and psychoanalytical) ideas have been incorporated into the theory and practice of numerous other approaches in the psychological, counselling, psychotherapeutic and associated fields, underlining its importance, influence and place in our professional world.

Summary

The psychodynamic approach has attained individuation from its parent, psychoanalysis. It has developed into a flexible, broader, more encompassing methodology. Modern psychodynamics is still evolving, wherein Attachment Theory and Object Relations are major features, the initial focus of practice being on client early experiences. It is commonly employed for long-term work, though a structured, short-term mode has been produced (usually of 15 sessions).

Psychodynamics is a respected and influential member of the counselling and psychotherapy family.

Learning Ideas

1   Consider the case of a single mother suffering from untreated post-natal depression, separated from her larger family, living on her own with a new-born baby. Think about possible attachment issues that might arise and how the child's development could be adversely affected. Write down your thoughts and include where you think a practitioner's boundaries are in such a case.

2   Honestly reflect on your early relationships. What have you brought into your adult relationships from your childhood attachments?

3   Revision

    a   Learn about Attachment Theory, child development and associated mental health issues, and how all this relates to adult relationships.

    b   Make sure you know the principles, structure and length of the short-term psychodynamic version.

    c   Be clear about the meanings and differences between: transference; displacement; projection; projective identification.

Suggested Reading

Coughlin Della Selva, P. (2004) *Intensive Short-Term Dynamic Psychotherapy.* London: Karnac Books.

Howard, S. (2011) *Psychodynamic Counselling in a Nutshell.* London: Sage.

Jacobs, M. (2007) *Psychodynamic Counselling in Action.* London: Sage.

12

Rational Emotive Behaviour Therapy (REBT)

Albert Ellis (1913–2007) was an American clinical psychologist, classical psychoanalyst, researcher and writer on diverse subjects including human sexuality. He became disillusioned with mainstream psychoanalysis, which maintained that adult psychological difficulties originate from early childhood. He was more concerned about how people's negative beliefs maintain their issues and problems rather than where the difficulties came from. This idea goes back into history to the ancient philosopher, Epictetus, who said that humans '...are not disturbed by things, but by the view they take of them'. Ellis also took inspiration from Stoicism, which says there are virtually no good reasons why human beings have to make themselves neurotic regardless of what negativities are impacting on them. Additionally, he was inspired by ideas from Buddhist philosophy, including those relating to logical reasoning.

From this, Ellis formed his foundation theory that it is self-defeating, negative thinking which causes what he termed *emotional disturbances*, by people not facing their irrational thinking processes. If they work at developing rational beliefs, then their emotions can become less disturbed and they will function better.

Ellis introduced Rational Therapy in the 1950s; roundabout 1961 he decided more recognition should be given to emotionality and its effects on our states of well-being, renaming the model Rational Emotive Therapy (RET). In 1993, after further deliberation, he produced the latest and clearest incarnation of his ideas, Rational Emotive Behaviour Therapy (REBT), acknowledging the importance of changing behaviours, cognitive, emotional and physical.

He influenced such as A.T. Beck (Cognitive Therapy), a major name in the sphere of psychological therapies.

Ellis believed human beings possess a strong inclination to think irrationally; this came from his observations of people having apparently unlimited capacities for distressing themselves. Interestingly, he also maintained that we have a fundamental tendency to think rationally about our irrationalities and so be in a position to reduce harmful effects of our counter-productive and disturbing cognitive processing. He stated that if we develop a rational philosophy of living, we can successfully combat the inclination towards irrationality and disturbed emotional states which inhibit our existence, while increasing our chances of *self-actualisation* (fulfilling our positive potential).

An important part of the philosophy just mentioned is for us to give up the negative *shoulds*, *oughts* and *musts* we carry, to minimise future psychological difficulties. In practice, there are clients who opt not to go the whole way concerning deeper change, choosing to take a less emphatic approach to disturbances, just reducing the severity of the negatives so they cope better than before. Ellis argued that such decisions leave underlying irrational beliefs in place and they may return to trouble the client again.

Extrapolating from this, he put forward three main REBT *insights*:

1　Irrational self-defeating beliefs create negative emotional states.
2　We accept and maintain these inhibiting beliefs because we have convinced ourselves (perhaps unconsciously) this is how things are and so the emotions are maintained.
3　We need to understand and accept that these negative beliefs can be overcome, although it requires practice, determination, effort and maybe a life-long challenge.

REBT theory suggests there are two forms of emotional disturbance underpinning neurotic issues:

1　Ego disturbance: this is when issues like guilt or shame affect us and we put ourselves under too much pressure (e.g., 'I didn't perform well in counselling practice so I must be rubbish') but overall we stay reality-based.
2　Discomfort disturbance: this is when we put unrealistic demands upon ourselves, others, or life, complaining that positive conditions should always exist for us, and we usually have low frustration tolerance (e.g., 'I can't take these coursework deadlines – they should be changed').

These disturbance types can overlap (e.g., blaming yourself as stupid (ego) for finding essays and projects stressful and difficult (discomfort)).

Ellis had an interesting view about *self-esteem*, a significant concept for practitioners from the mass of counselling approaches. He saw self-esteem as a type of judgement and valuing of a person which comes from external validation objects (e.g., people, possessions, jobs, qualifications, achievements). The contention is that if these are threatened or lost then self-esteem can be negatively affected, so it's seen as temporary or fluctuational. Ellis and REBT prefer to concentrate on assisting people achieve *unconditional self-acceptance*, where a person refuses to be adversely impacted by extraneous life events, and it's considered a stronger foundation for functional living.

Another set of REBT concepts are:

- Awfulising: gauging events as more negative than they really are; think of over-reaction or exaggeration.
- Damning: being overly critical of self or other people or life.
- Low frustration tolerance (LFT): when a person perceives disturbance in their life and judges themselves incapable of overcoming it and changing things.

These ideas illustrate irrational and self-defeating thinking and beliefs because they lack rational reasoning and are unrealistic. Ellis set out to help clients change unhealthy, and even dysfunctional, emotions into healthier ones via the process of *belief change*.

Relating to this, he initially introduced the *ABC* format to explain how negative thinking affects and disturbs our emotions (see Chapter 5 on Cognitive Therapy) but in the 1980s he extended this concept into the *ABCDE* model of understanding emotional disturbance, development and thinking:

A: activating event (perceived negative experience, actual or imagined).
B: beliefs (self-defeating thinking).
C: consequences (emotional, behavioural and physical).
D: disputing irrational beliefs: challenging and disproving negative thoughts and beliefs.
E: effective new philosophy, the result of becoming more rational.

Ellis suggested that we accept ourselves as we are, i.e., imperfect human beings. He said it's OK to feel negative emotions, but he encouraged people not to over-react or exaggerate their power.

Some Big Names

Dryden, W. (1970s onwards): British psychotherapist; he developed Rational Emotive Cognitive Behaviour Therapy (RECBT); first professor of counselling in the UK.

Ellis, D.J. (1990s onwards): American wife of Ellis; psychologist, mental health counsellor, alternative/holistic practitioner; worked with Ellis on training and research projects.

Hulbeck, C.R. (1892–1974): German Jungian psychoanalyst who moved to America; he was analyst and supervisor of Ellis.

Rogers, C.R. (1902–1987): American psychologist and psychotherapist; influential in developing humanistic thinking which interested Ellis.

Some Big Ideas

Rational-emotive imagery; unconditional self-acceptance; insight; client self-empowerment; practitioner redundancy.

How it Works

REBT has a range of techniques to facilitate rational thinking and change: cognitive, behavioural, emotive and imagery. These techniques are employed to help clients examine and assess irrational beliefs by the use of *realism*, *logic* and *usefulness*, and then replace them with more rational and realistic ones, so reducing emotional disturbance in order to live better.

At the outset of counselling, clients are informed of what their role is in the process so they can make the most of it. This involves them understanding and accepting that emotional disturbances are largely self-induced and sustained. Furthermore, they need to comprehend and accept that homework-task completion and actions by them are required to constructively alter the way they have become.

The process commences with an assessment in order to see how client issues fit with the ABCDE construction, which is the introduction to client self-understanding. At this stage both practitioner and client may not be fully aware of how deep the issues go, and this is revealed via *inference chaining*, where the client's negative beliefs are linked together.

Future sessions are based around agreed agendas which include the review of the previous session and homework, deciding on work for the current meeting, plus resulting homework tasks. The client is encouraged to give feedback about how each session has been for them.

Agendas are considered to be important for structure and time-efficiency, helping to retain a focus on the therapeutic goals.

 A brief example

A new client suffers from anxiety, which affects all areas of their life (late 20s, single, employed full-time, shares a flat with a friend): 'I'm a bit of a worrier.' They want to feel more at ease with themselves and 'not get so stressed about everything'.

After the assessment, you employ person-centred *core conditions* to help create rapport and establish trust in the client so they feel safe enough to start exploring their issues with you. The initial focus is on the client's friendship group; *ego disturbance* is expressed with the client believing that if they don't conform to group desires they will be rejected, proving they are unlikeable, which makes them feel anxious. The client is also affected by *discomfort disturbance* in this context, getting upset if friends don't contact them at agreed times: 'I always ring or text when I say I will, but the others don't. I can't stand it when that happens and I shouldn't be treated like that – it's so unfair!'

When you hear such comments you might be tempted to connect your client's anxieties to low self-esteem, a result of childhood experiences, as many practitioners from other approaches would. However, using an REBT perspective, you focus on *acceptance* issues, exploring your client's tendencies to *awfulise* the situation regarding the friendship group, their *low frustration tolerance* at the friends' lack of consideration, and the group and themselves for not being perfect (e.g., the friends' lack of punctuality and thoughtfulness, and their own passivity), and, in fact, 'the world' for not being reasonable to the client. Additionally, the client wants to talk about their relationship with a powerful parent but you explain that REBT tends not to focus on early attachments. They agree to stay focused on what directly brought them to you.

Your relationship with the client grows as you show empathy, unconditional positive regard, genuineness, trustworthiness and competence with fundamental counselling skills. The client opens up and, utilising the *ABCDE* model, you reach a stage where you can dispute the client about their unlikeability and challenge their 'shoulds'.

The positive dynamic leads to the client thinking more rationally until they accept emotionally as well as intellectually that situations, such as late phone calls from friends, do not equate to rejection and unlikeability. This is *belief change* happening. In addition, they begin to ease up on themselves by not always being immediately available to others, i.e., allowing themselves to be 'imperfect'.

As progress continues the client starts to assert themselves with their friends, sometimes expressing different desires and preferences; they discover this *doesn't* end in group rejection and unlikeability. The client learns to accept that they, other people, the world, can all be imperfect without catastrophic results occurring. Further, their inclinations to over-react and negatively exaggerate decline, establishing an enhanced, constructive way of thinking, emoting and managing themselves in life.

Who it's For

Research has found REBT to be useful for: generalised anxiety; social anxiety; exam anxiety; speech anxiety; anger; temper tantrums; depression; those with suicidal thoughts; shy/withdrawn adolescents; young children who have difficulty making friends and acting socially; people with long-term anti-social behaviours; aiding emotionally healthy people cope better with daily stresses. Thus, it can be effective with young people and older individuals.

As with many therapies REBT may not work with individuals who won't stop blaming others for their negative feelings, and clients who won't do the necessary amount of work to gain control over their issues.

Critical Considerations

There is experimental evidence to suggest that REBT is effective at reducing emotional disturbance; in fact, it's one of the most studied modalities. However, Ellis himself criticised some research for being too narrow in which aspects of REBT they examined.

Some critics say the model is too confrontational for certain people, though this has been refuted by others who point to the inclusion of person-centred principles for establishing sound therapeutic relationships between practitioners and clients. We should note here that mediocre practitioners from any approach can be inappropriately confrontational with clients.

It's also been argued that the approach is too inflexible and fails to address deep, underlying issues. Again, this is disputed, REBT theorists saying deeper work can be done, bearing in mind that practitioners work with what clients want to focus on. Flexibility is possible, too, as the model is adaptable to individual client needs. Moreover, Ellis accepted challenges to his work, acknowledged errors and revised his theories and practice accordingly.

Identifying Features

REBT can be utilised for both short-term and longer-term work; it incorporates cognitive, behavioural and psychodynamic features, while acknowledging the importance of core conditions from person-centred philosophy; it's one of the most widely-used approaches around the world.

Reflections

In my view, REBT stands out from the crowd of cognitive behavioural methodologies that have appeared over the last 40–50 years. I think a major strength is the integration of psychodynamic, cognitive and behavioural concepts, aligned with a person-centred base. It is structured and theoretically well grounded, while being flexible to individual needs, drawing from this broad range of therapeutic perspectives.

On a personal note, I learned to utilise an REBT approach in relation to my own self-management concerning personal and professional development, which explains part of my appreciation of the model.

The approach probably isn't so applicable to clients wanting an in-depth exploration and understanding of their state of being, for which perhaps a psychodynamic, Gestalt, Existential or Person-Centred process could be more suitable.

Summary

REBT is considered by many theorists as the original cognitive behavioural therapy. It's well grounded, with significant research support. The method can work at depth with younger and older people with a diversity of issues and conditions, although it is mostly employed in shorter-term counselling. It is taught worldwide.

Learning Ideas

1   Explore your view on REBT's perspective on self-acceptance versus self-esteem; make sure you understand the differences between the two concepts. Then write down the definitions of the two terms and what your thinking is on this topic.
2   How could you utilise REBT to improve your own self-management on an everyday basis?
3   Revision

    a   Make sure you know how and why Rational Therapy developed into Rational Emotive Therapy and then Rational Emotive Behaviour Therapy.

    b   Learn the fundamentals of Stoicism and how it relates to REBT.

    c   Check out and understand Windy Dryden's Rational Emotive Cognitive Behavioural Therapy (RECBT).

 **Suggested Reading**

Dryden, W. and Neenan, M. (2004) *Counselling Individuals: A Rational Emotive Behavioural Handbook* (4th edition). Chichester: Wiley.

Ellis, A. (2004) *Rational Emotive Behaviour Therapy: It Works for Me – It Can Work for You.* New York: Prometheus Books.

Thorburn, R. (2011) *Rational Emotive Behaviour Therapy.* Washington, DC: American Psychological Association.

13

Transactional Analysis (TA)

Eric Berne (1910–1970) was an American psychiatrist who studied psychoanalysis under Paul Federn before further study with Eric Erikson. Berne extended Federn's Ego-State Model and gradually diverged from the mainstream of psychoanalytical thought. His work developed and Transactional Analysis (TA) was the result, introduced in the 1950s. He said verbal communication is at the centre of psychoanalysis and human social relationships.

Berne wanted a theory that could be easily understood and available to everyone, and the approach outlines how we develop into who we are, how we communicate and relate to others, offering ideas and interventions to enable change and growth.

His general aim was for TA to aid clients to free themselves from negativities founded in childhood so they can function and relate better with other people.

TA is now usually classed among humanistic approaches to personal change because of its emphasis on personal responsibility, an equal relationship between practitioner and client, and the intrinsic worth of the person. It shares some characteristics with the behavioural approach, especially regarding contract-making, combining comfortably with ideas from the psychoanalytical tradition.

The International Transactional Analysis Association defines TA as a systematic psychotherapy for personal growth and change, and a theory of personality. Others describe it as a neo- or extra-Freudian personality theory. Another way of considering the approach is as a social psychology, and a method to improve communication.

TA takes an assertive view of the possibility of personal growth and constructive change. An individual will achieve this not merely by gaining insight into their old patterns of behaviour, but by deciding to change those patterns and taking action to achieve goals.

TA has three main assumptions:

1 People are OK.
2 Everyone has the capacity to think (except obvious exceptions, e.g., those with certain brain injuries or degenerative brain conditions).
3 People actually decide their own destiny and these decisions can be changed.

Berne said if we are able to think, it's the responsibility of each of us to decide what we want from life, and individuals will ultimately live with the consequences of their decisions.

Initially, Berne wanted to *cure* clients and not simply help them progress. However, as his theories developed he had another way of defining 'cure', proposing the idea that the goal of personal change is *autonomy* (implying the ability to rationally solve problems and resolve issues in the here-and-now reality). The components of autonomy are awareness, spontaneity and the capacity for intimacy or personal relationships. In this, the cure, or move to autonomous living, is a progressive process involving four stages:

1 Social control.
2 Symptomatic relief.
3 Transference cure (transference pertaining to the Parent–Adult–Child role relationship concept).
4 Script cure.

These days TA practitioners have differing views about what constitutes cure, some simply equating it with completion of the therapeutic contract....

Berne related interpersonal relationships and communication to three *ego states*, the Parent–Adult–Child (PAC) format:

- Parent: this pertains to our social learning, conditioning, attitude development, feelings, beliefs and behaviours; it is the voice of authority in our heads.
- Child: our internal reactions, feelings and emotions from external events form this dimension; we tend to replay emotions, thoughts and behaviours learned in childhood.
- Adult: this part represents our ability to think rationally and decide for ourselves; it's the guide to better functioning and needs to be strong enough to change and handle the Parent and Child states.

The PAC construct is a way of understanding our psychological structuring, suggesting how we function and express our personality via our behaviours. In other words, it explains how life patterns originate in childhood and we replay them as adults even if results are negative. In this way it also offers a theory of psychopathology.

A very important concept here is *structural analysis*, the process of analysing personality in terms of ego states.

In 1964, Berne's classic book *Games People Play* was published, reinforcing his presence in the therapeutic sphere, bringing TA to a mass audience, which was his intention.

Following this, in 1969, one of Berne's associates, T.A. Harris, released his book *I'm OK, You're OK*. He proposed that each of us has four thought-based *life positions* which are employed in our relationships, communications and interactions with other people:

1 I'm Not OK, You're OK.
2 I'm Not OK, You're Not OK.
3 I'm OK, You're Not OK.
4 I'm OK, You're OK.

The book became an international bestseller, helping to bring the fundamentals of TA to the general public. It also contributed to the criticism that the approach was just a simplistic 'pop psychology'. Nevertheless, it continues to be sold in large numbers to the present day, on the back of TA's resurgence as a serious contributor to human growth, communication and improved functioning.

From the 1980s particularly, the original TA has evolved, with new variations forming the basis of work conducted by most modern practitioners. In 2010/2011, Anita Mountain and Chris Davidson of Mountain Associates (Desford, UK) produced the Transactional Analysis OK Modes Model (*mode* differentiates the behaviour categories from the earlier structural ego-state model mentioned above). There are 10 Modes with a central *Mindfulness Process*; this refers to communicating 'OK to OK' messages, i.e., constructively in the here-and-now, responding appropriately rather than ineffectively and destructively. This new model views the three ego states as follows:

- Parent:
  nurturing (nurturing – positive; spoiling – negative)
  controlling (structuring – positive; critical – negative)
- (Integrated) Adult: remains as it was in the early theory, drawing on the resources of the other two dimensions.

- Child:
  adapted (cooperative – positive; compliant/resistant – negative)
  free (spontaneous – positive; immature – negative)

The most effective transactions (successful communications) are Adult to Adult.

It's worth noting here there are three schools of TA, dating from the 1970s:

1 The Classical school, which adheres to Berne's original ideas.
2 The Redecision school, which believes it's OK to initially work with clients in their Child before helping them develop into their Adult.
3 The Cathexis school, which has similarities with the Redecision school but where the practitioner actively assumes the role of 'parent'; they become a new, more appropriate parent than the client originally perceived they had.

▬▬▬ Some Big Names ▬▬▬

Federn, P. (1871–1950): tutor of Berne; into social psychology and treatment of psychosis via therapy; he produced the ego-state model.

Harris, T.A. (1950s onwards): follower of Berne; he became Director of the International TA Association.

Karpman, S. (1960s onwards): leading TA theorist; he produced the Drama Triangle model, which refers to psychological roles people might take in a communication dynamic, i.e., one is *victim*, another is *persecutor*, and the third is *rescuer*.

Steiner, C. (born 1935): he developed the idea of the *stroke economy*, which says that as children we learn that there can be restrictive rules about strokes, relating to the concept of conditional approval from parent/authority figures.

Some Big Ideas

Practitioner–client contract; life positions; 'blame' model; (life) scripts; closing escape hatches; injunctions and drivers (dos and don'ts); time structuring; games; rackets.

How it Works

TA is an action-based approach to personal change. The practitioner doesn't assume the therapeutic relationship of itself will necessarily bring about that change. Instead, they develop a *script analysis* of the client via a *script questionnaire*, examining the client's life script, then jointly produce a flexible contract and treatment direction for changes to be made. The practitioner intervenes in a planned and structured manner to help achieve the agreed goals. This involves the 3Ps, i.e., giving clients *permission* to go against the critical Parent in their heads, showing clients they have more *potency* than the critical voice, and *protecting* (supporting) clients from the internal Parent until they can protect themselves.

The guiding principle for clients is that if we analyse ourselves and others in interactions, we produce better chances of understanding more clearly what's happening and choosing how to communicate with other people. If we learn to make the most of our communications, this is fundamental to creating, developing and maintaining improved relationships.

A brief example

(Following the Classical school which stays with Berne's original thinking, the practitioner communicating to the client in 'I'm OK, You're OK' manner, i.e., Adult to Adult.)
A new client suffers from anxiety, which affects all areas of their life (late 20s, single, employed full-time, shares a flat with a friend): 'I'm a bit of a worrier.' They want to feel more at ease with themselves and 'not get so stressed about everything'.

Initially, you allow the client to discuss what brings them here and explore more closely the development of their *life script*, including messages picked up from primary carers in childhood, using your script questionnaire. Discuss the *closing escape hatches* part of the contract (the client makes and states a decision not to go crazy, nor harm or kill themselves or anyone else) as you move towards this jointly-produced agreement for the work. As you learn more about the client you might make contract alterations. Be supportive, encouraging and empowering so the client develops confidence that life-long beliefs from the unhelpful internal Parent can be faced and overcome, and that they have the strength to become their own Adult, not being dominated by their Child and negative Parent.

Perhaps you and the client conclude that parental messages such as 'The world is a risky, scary place', and 'People judge you, so watch how you behave, and don't upset them, because then they won't like you', are fundamental to the client's interactions with people and situations.

You support the client to reflect on such messages and the impact they can have on a developing individual. Additionally, it allows you time to ponder the nature of the client's early relationships and gain understanding that maybe they have learnt to be a 'worrier' from an anxious parent. This can be empowering for the client, particularly one who may feel disloyal at apparently criticising a person who loves them. They can work with the idea that understanding and rejecting inhibiting messages doesn't mean they are criticising or betraying their parent or anyone else. From here they begin to reconsider their inner Parent voice and messages, thinking in their strengthening Adult, gradually taking control of the Child inside them and reducing anxiety, leading to improved functioning.

Who it's For

The approach is used in numerous settings: e.g., mental health, including some forms of psychosis; organisational (e.g., to develop more functional relationships); educational (e.g., better parenting, student motivation, staff morale); social work; families (e.g., couples work); communications training.

It can be applied to people of all ages and across cultures in short-term or longer contexts.

Critical Considerations

TA was developed to be an easily understood, non-technical approach for non-professionals; more recently its concepts have been integrated into the work of practitioners from other perspectives.

T.A. Harris claimed scientific support for the approach from experiments conducted by Wilder Penfield, an early pioneer of neurology and brain surgery, who discovered strong emotional childhood memories could be relived in adulthood.

TA has been criticised as simplistic and suffered from media 'popularisation', becoming denigrated by many mainstream theoreticians in its early years.

'Cure' is a contentious topic, as are some of the later definitions of the term, e.g., as completion of a contract.

The Redecision and Cathexis schools could be criticised for collusion, dependency and strengthening the Child at the expense of the Adult.

The concept of *closed escape hatches* speaks to non-suicide/violence contracts with clients and is criticised for being essentially pointless.

Identifying Features

TA has foundations in the psychoanalytical and behavioural traditions plus a strong cognitive dimension; it's intended to demystify therapeutic language so we can all access and understand it better; when considered as a communication theory, it's adaptable to analysing systems and organisations.

Reflections

While TA followers clearly acknowledge its foundations in psychoanalytical and behavioural theories, I continue to be slightly puzzled by the apparent lack of formal recognition of the patently strong cognitive dimension.

A basic tenet of the approach focuses on our ability to think; from this we can change negative thinking and improve our decision-making in order to better function in the future. Therefore, why isn't this dimension formally presented as an integral foundation of TA?

The essentials of TA, e.g., client responsibility for their decisions, actions and consequences, are consistent with other models and can certainly be accommodated in an integrative approach. Many of my colleagues and supervisees have been able to utilise the PAC ego states in their work after gaining comprehension of the approach. In addition, clients have reported improved self-awareness, understanding and management after learning and implementing these concepts, e.g., 'When I was speaking to my partner I went straight into Child mode. Then I realised what I was doing and made myself become the Adult, which helped us not argue.'

Summary

Berne wanted TA to be an approach that everyone could understand and learn to use on themselves. It draws on two founding therapeutic schools of thought while coming under the description of being humanistic in nature. The development of Berne's theories led to marginalisation from the historical psychoanalytic tradition, TA being ostracised for some time. It's now regained its position and continues to evolve.

Learning Ideas

1   Reflect on and write down your thoughts about Berne's assertion that we all decide our own destiny (focus on the psychological dimension – don't jump to the 'What happens if you get knocked down by a car? That's not your own decision', defence). Be as open and honest with yourself as you can.
2   How strong are your Child and Parent compared to your Adult, and when does each ego state tend to operate?
3   Revision:

    a   Compare and contrast the original PAC Model with the later version and decide how different they are from each other.

> b Consider the changing definitions of the term 'cure' in TA and how useful they are. Then decide how 'cure' sits with you in your training.
>
> c Consider how meaningful it is to have a client agree not to go crazy during sessions.

Suggested Reading

Erskine, R.G. (2010) *Life Scripts: A Transactional Analysis of Unconscious Relational Patterns.* London: Karnac Books.

Stewart, I. (2007) *Transactional Counselling in Action.* London: Sage.

Tudor, K. (2001) *Transactional Approaches to Brief Therapy: Or, What Do You Say between Saying Hello and Goodbye?* London: Sage.

14
At the End...

My Post Graduate Diploma in Counselling laid a firm foundation for my professional work in this field. The memory of the course and my early years as a practitioner are as clear as ever, and I empathise with those undertaking training and establishing themselves in counselling and psychotherapy.

After graduation I still had much to reflect on in terms of both my professional and personal development, plus uncertainties and questions about aspects of practice. As I settled into the profession, then related roles, I found these uncertainties and questions in colleagues, students and supervisees too. In this chapter I share some of these topics in case they are of any interest or use to you as students or qualified practitioners.

Your Own Therapy

On most diploma programmes I know course components include a required number of personal counselling sessions that students should have in preparation for being a professional practitioner. Some students approach this part of their course as no more than an assessable item as opposed to an integral factor in becoming ready for practice. Others more clearly understand the nature and purpose of going for their own therapy, remaining open to having more than their training programme demands if it seems necessary or desirable. I believe this is a good sign in an aspiring professional.

When you search for a therapist it might be worthwhile to look for one who works from your own theoretical perspective. Please allow yourself the right to request seeing their diplomas and certificates, and not simply a CV. If they take your request negatively, then go somewhere else....

In some countries it's heavily encouraged that practitioners should be in therapy throughout their career. Another view contends that such a demand ignores concepts like *dependency* and *practitioner self-reliance*. I am of the general view that we should undergo our own counselling in preparation for professional practice and be prepared to return in the future should we need to.

To be a good practitioner, in my view, involves working on your self-awareness. However, that's only the first step; I think self-awareness has its limitations in this context unless it leads to self-development so we can become better at what we do. Vital qualities here are *self-honesty*, *courage* and *discipline*, with which to explore yourself deeply and openly in order to attain *professional self-actualisation*, for want of a better term. Others might equate these qualities to *integrity*, too.

Clinical Supervision

In some countries once students have qualified they aren't required to have supervision when in practice. In others, e.g., the UK, practitioners are, at the very least, heavily encouraged to have regular supervision for the duration of their careers. This is certainly my strongly-held view.

In the UK, as a student it's common to have one hour of clinical supervision for every five client sessions (the norm being 50 minutes as the definition of a therapeutic client hour). Currently, the BACP guidelines (British Association of Counselling and Psychotherapy) suggest a qualified practitioner should have a minimum of 1.5 hours per month, although it doesn't state how many sessions this should encompass. As an experienced clinical supervisor for over 20 years, I encourage professional practitioners to work with a ratio of 1:8, i.e., one hour of supervision for every eight client sessions.

When seeking and meeting a potential supervisor it might be advisable to find one who has the same theoretical orientation as you, particularly if you've only just qualified. Additionally, feel free to ask to see their documents (diplomas, certificates, etc.). Don't be satisfied with a CV and what they tell you about their qualifications. It's your right, in my opinion, to know what they actually have to offer. In my experience and that of friends and colleagues, competent and confident supervisors aren't offended by such enquiries. If a prospective supervisor gets huffy or precious about such a request, then maybe that's telling you something, and you should go elsewhere....

It seems the dominating perspective is that a practitioner should receive clinical supervision for the duration of their career in the field, and I share this standpoint.

Beginnings of Practice with Each Client

I've included some basic *dos* and *don'ts* for practitioners when starting out, in no particular order:

- The first meeting/phone call/leaflet: explain about such as: your theoretical orientation; length of sessions; fees and payments; cancellation procedures; client lateness.

- Emergencies: in private practice *you* define what constitutes a situation where a client might contact you 'out of hours'. Of course, you might decide not to offer such a facility, which is sometimes easier said than done when you consider clients have your contact details. If you counsel for an organisation on premises, ensure there's a protocol surrounding client emergencies, what defines them and that clients are made aware of it.

- Confidentiality: a general rule is that everything is confidential unless you assess that a client is a risk to themselves or another person, or the client is at risk from someone else.

- An initial assessment/client profile: in private practice make sure you take the pertinent details from a client (e.g., contact details in case you have to cancel a session; a client's next of kin/emergency contact person and their details; GP contact details; whether the client has been in counselling before; what brings them to therapy *now*; what they want from counselling).

- If a client doesn't turn up: the general rule is it's their responsibility to let you know if they're not arriving. If they don't do this, it's *not* for you to contact them to find out why they didn't come; this could be seen as chasing them…. They could have any number of reasons for not attending or informing you, and you don't want to be seen as hassling them by seeking them out for an explanation. If you find yourself tempted to do such a thing, reflect on what's driving you to do so and take it to supervision, your tutor or placement manager if that's where it happens. Some counselling services, e.g., in the Voluntary/Community sector, might have procedures for contacting non-arrivals, particularly if there's a waiting list and sessions are at a premium. In such scenarios, they could consider it a priority to discover whether a non-attender will be back or has concluded therapy without informing the agency. Many such services prefer to write letters or use email rather than spending time following the client by phone.

Charging and Collecting Fees

Here are a few pointers and ideas to consider should you be in a context of receiving payment for your work in private practice. It is very common to be paid for a number of sessions in advance, say four. If a particular client has difficulty with the amount of fees this entails, then some of us might accept payment for three sessions in advance, or even two. Prior to this, it is common practice to conduct a one-off assessment and ask to be paid in cash – cheques have been known to bounce!

There are some psychodynamic training programmes which guide their graduates to arrange for fees to be paid in arrears. Explained in simple terms, the rationale for this guidance derives from a belief that practitioners will have issues (e.g., guilt feelings) about charging people for services, plus the fact that there can be difficulties in gaining rightful remunerations from someone once they have received counselling. The contention is that a practitioner should experience the struggle of obtaining owed fees from clients, and work through the issues involved. For example, suppose such a client misses an appointment: when you seek the agreed fees they might resist paying for the one they missed: 'I wasn't here, so I don't see why I should have to pay for the session.' This can happen even if you set out your rules about missing sessions and the required amount of notice to be given in order not to have to pay for the meeting in question. Bear in mind, if you are operating from a psychodynamic viewpoint, that you might be expecting clients to pay for all missed sessions, no matter what the reason is.... So, if you are from this perspective and a client can't come for four sessions (or eight, or 15 – you get the picture!) and they are supposed to pay in arrears, consider the 'interesting' discussions you could have if you ask them to pay for all the absences, even if it was due to, say, a broken leg or illness or death in their family. Good luck with that...!

Here's a straightforward approach: a one-off assessment paid in cash; a standard four sessions in advance with some flexibility, but a bottom-line of two sessions upfront; if given 24 hours notice of a cancellation, the client doesn't 'lose' the session. If, for some reason, the practitioner should have to cancel a session then, of course, the client won't lose out financially.

If you join an organisation which charges fees, then make sure part of your induction includes the rules, guidelines and procedures they use for gathering payments from clients (including clients' employers).

Relationship Boundaries with Clients

- While it's important to be welcoming to a client, always remember it's a professional relationship you're embarking on – you're not working with clients to become their friend. That means you don't start swapping anecdotes or telling them about yourself, family, work, hobbies, holidays, illnesses or the fact you're very tired this week!
- If you see a client in the street and they see you, don't hide, run away, pretend you haven't noticed or otherwise ignore them; just smile, say hello and keep walking.
- A difficult issue for some (new) practitioners concerns time boundaries with clients, including such as early arrivals and the lateness of clients turning up for sessions.

For many, a therapeutic hour is usually 50 minutes long, although some do work with 60 minutes. Couples work can vary between 60 and 75 minutes per session. Group sessions often vary between one and two hours (and can include a 15–20-minute break).

Now I'll give you a few things to reflect on by presenting a real-life example. A clinical supervisor colleague of mine reported a situation they would have to deal with on this subject while I was producing this final chapter.

The following illustration is about how *not* to be good with time boundaries. A practitioner had booked in a client for a 1 o'clock session, to last 50 minutes.

> 1.05pm: the practitioner received a phone call from the client saying they'd be about 15 minutes late.

1.20pm: the client called again saying they'd be arriving at about 1.40pm. The practitioner was heard to reply, 'That's fine, don't worry about it.'
1.45pm: the client finally turned up five minutes before the official end of the session. The practitioner made them both tea and the session commenced at 1.49pm.
3.01: the session ended.

To sum up, a 50-minute session was supposed to commence at 1 o'clock but started one minute before it should have finished. The actual session lasted for 72 minutes because the practitioner allowed it to run over time (no, it wasn't an emergency).

It might be an idea for you to reflect on the practitioner issues and actions underlying this scenario because you need to be clear and disciplined about time boundaries, flexibility, asserting yourself with clients, length of sessions and keeping to agreed time-frames.

Consider this question: when might an appointment become pointless in terms of client lateness – 20, 25, 35 minutes into the 50-minute session?

A final observation for you relating to the example above: the practitioner in this case was also a clinical supervisor to four students...

Couples/Pairs/Group-work

At the end of my Post Grad Diploma I asked my tutor about this as part of my professional development. I believe she gave me some particularly sound guidance when she said I should get a good five years experience of one-to-one work before considering anything else. Furthermore, she advised that anyone without couples training should get some before embarking on such work. In addition, she said a practitioner should discuss the prospect with their clinical supervisor and get their view of the practitioner's readiness for this area of work. Similarly, the guidance was to gain some solid experience with pairs before considering groups, if that's an ambition for someone. Again, a group-work qualification was advised.

Her ideas have always held me in good stead and I see no reason to advise others differently. Remember, good practitioners know their current limitations as well as their strengths so 'don't run before you can walk'.

Endings with Clients

I was taught about endings in the context of long-term work with clients. Let's suppose the therapy has lasted for 90 weekly sessions over a two-year period. The client has attended regularly so there have been no attendance issues and progress has been made. You and the client have jointly concluded that it's time to draw counselling to a close but you keep the door open in case they need to return in the future. You have discussed endings over the last 15 sessions or so, giving time for both parties to talk about topics like loss, sadness, anxiety, progress mainte-nance and relapse prevention. All has gone smoothly and now you're at the stage when the ending 'starts'.

1   Move to having a session every two weeks for two months.
2   Next, have a session every three weeks for six weeks.
3   Then one session per month for two months.

Many courses don't have much guidance about endings so this model at least gives you something to consider as a basic process for concluding your work with a client.

Some research evidence to ponder if you are thinking of becoming a practitioner:

1   Counselling and psychotherapy can make constructive changes in people's lives.

2   It would seem that the main deciding factor in the effectiveness of our work is the active commitment of the client.... Bear that in mind if you tend to be self-critical about your abilities when training or in professional practice (Cooper, 2011).

At the end of this Guide I find myself thinking about what motivated me to write it. The main reason is that I wanted to make a contribution to helping practitioners become as good as possible at what they do and provide quality services to clients.

In counselling and psychotherapy terms, the following components are to be found in quality practitioners: appropriate levels of qualifications and training; a broad and deep range of knowledge, experience, and competencies; attitudes and behaviours that indicate such as empathy, respect, non-judgementalism, acceptance of others. To conclude, self-awareness and self-development are critical factors requiring self-honesty, discipline, integrity and perhaps courage. I'll leave you to ponder that.

Finally, I include a simple summarised information and comparison table of salient factors to aid your learning about the approaches described in this Guide.

I wish you well.

TABLE

APPROACH	FOUNDERS/ LEADERS	DATE OF ORIGIN	MODE	THEORETICAL BASE	DURATION	AGES	CONTEXT
Behaviour Therapy	B.F. Skinner, H.J. Eysenck, J. Wolpe	1920s	Single	Behaviourism	Short-term	Any	Mental health, education, animal training
Cognitive Analytical Therapy (CAT)	A. Ryle, A.L. Brown, L.S. Vygotsky	Late 1970s	Integrated	Cognitive psychology, Psychoanalysis	Short-term	Any	Mental health, general settings
Cognitive Behaviour Therapy (CBT)	A.T. Beck, A. Ellis, A. Lazarus, A. Bandura	1970–1990s	Integrated	Cognitive Therapy, Behaviour Therapy	Short-term	Any	Mental health, education, workplace, general
Cognitive Therapy	A.T. Beck, A. Ellis, G. Kelly	1960s	Single then integrated	Cognitive, then integrated Behavioural ideas	Usually short-term	Any	Mental health, education
Developmental Counselling	G. Egan, R. Carkhuff, S. Gilmore, E. Erikson	Mid-1970s	Integrated	PCA, Cognitive, Behavioural ideas	Usually longer-term	Any	Education, workplace, mental health, general
Existential Counselling	M. Heidegger R.D. Laing, E. van Deurzen-Smith [Ed?]	Early 1920s	Integrated	Existential philosophy, phenomenology, PCA	Longer-term	Adults	General settings

APPROACH	FOUNDERS/ LEADERS	DATE OF ORIGIN	MODE	THEORETICAL BASE	DURATION	AGES	CONTEXT
Gestalt Therapy	F. Perls, E. & M. Polster, R.F. Hefferline	1920s	Single	Gestalt psychology, Existentialism, Humanistic psychology	Usually longer-term	Any	Anxiety, phobias, depression, workplace, coaching
Integrative Counselling	S. Culley, D. Nelson-Jones	1990s	Integrated/ eclectic	Humanistic psychology, PCA	Longer-term	Any	General settings
Person-Centred Counselling (PCA)	C. Rogers, O. Rank, E.H. Porter, C. Devonshire	1940s	Single	Humanistic psychology, philosophy	Longer-term	Any	Mental health, education, families, general
Psychodynamic Counselling and Psychotherapy	M. Klein, D. Winnicott, W.R. Bion, J.M. Bowlby	1940s	Single	Psychoanalysis	Usually longer-term	Any	Mental health, education, families, general settings
Rational Emotive Behaviour Therapy (REBT)	A. Ellis, W. Dryden	Early 1990s	Integrated	Psychoanalysis, Cognitive Therapy, Behaviour Therapy	Usually short-term	Any	General, eg. anxiety, depression
Transactional Analysis (TA)	E. Berne, P. Federn, T.A. Harris	1950s	Integrated	Psychoanalysis, Cognitive psychology, Humanistic psychology	Short- and longer-term	Any	Mental health, education, families, management

An A4 version of this table is available to download from www.sagepub.co.uk/pennington

Bibliography

Berne, E. (1964) *Games People Play: The Basic Hand Book of Transactional Analysis*. New York: Grove Press.

Brooks-Harris, J.E. (2008) *Integrative Multitheoretical Psychotherapy*. Boston, MA: Houghton-Mifflin.

Brownell, P. (ed.) (2008) *The Handbook for Theory, Research and Practice in Gestalt Therapy*. Newcastle on Tyne: Cambridge Scholars Publishing.

Clark, D.A. and Beck, A.T. (2010) *Cognitive Therapy of Anxiety Disorders: Science and Practice*. New York: Guilford Press.

Colman, A.M. (2001) *Oxford Dictionary of Psychology*. New York and Oxford: Oxford University Press.

Cooper, M. (2011) *Essential Research Findings in Counselling and Psychotherapy*. London: Sage.

Cooper, M., O'Hara, M., Schmid, P. and Wyatt, G. (2007) *The Handbook of Person-Centred Psychotherapy*. London: Palgrave Macmillan.

Egan, G. (2004) *The Skilled Helper*. Pacific Grove, CA; Wadsworth. **(Developmental Counselling)**

Etchegoyen, H. (2005) *The Fundamentals of Psychoanalytic Technique*. London: Karnac Books.

Farber, B.A. (1998) *The Psychotherapy of Carl Rogers: Cases and Commentary*. New York: Guilford Press.

Harris, T.A. (1969) *I'm Ok, You're Ok*. New York: Harper Collins. **(Transactional Analysis)**

Hergenhahn, B.R. (2005) *An Introduction to the History of Psychology*. Belmont, CA: Thomson Wadsworth.

Houston, G. (2003) *Brief Gestalt Therapy*. London: Sage.

McLeod, J. (1994) *Doing Counselling Research*. London: Sage.

Mills, J.A. (2000) *Control: A History of Behavioural Psychology*. New York: New York University Press.

Palmer, S. (2000) *Introduction to Counselling and Psychotherapy*. London: Sage.

Palmer, S. and Woolfe, R. (1999) *Integrative and Eclectic Counselling and Psychotherapy*. London: Sage.

Rogers, C. (1961) *On Becoming a Person: A Therapist's View of Psychotherapy*. London: Constable. (**Rogerian philosophy/the Person-Centred Approach**)

Roget, P.M. (1982) *Roget's Thesaurus*. London: Longman.

Schneider, K.J. (2011) Existential–Humanistic Therapies. In S.B. Messer and A. Gurman (eds), *Essential Psychotherapies* (3rd edition). New York: Guilford Press.

Timulak, L. (2008) *Research in Psychotherapy and Counselling*. London: Sage.

Index

155